Life
Gardener

Life Gardener

SEED, PLANT AND GROW YOUR FULL BLOOM LIFE

LYNDAL EDWARDS

LifeGardener: Seed, Plant & Grow Your Full Bloom Life

Copyright © Lyndal Edwards, First published 2022

Lyndal Edwards asserts the moral right to be identified as the author of

LifeGardener: Seed, Plant & Grow Your Full Bloom Life

Copyright © Blossom Books Publishing

All rights reserved. No part of this publication may be reproduced, stored in a retrieval system or transmitted in any form or by any means, mechanical, electronic, photocopying, recording or otherwise, without the prior written permission of the author.

This book and any associated materials, suggestions and advice are intended to give general information only. The author expressly disclaims all liability to any person arising directly or indirectly from the use of, or for any errors or omissions in this book. The adoption and application of the information in this book is at the readers' discretion and is his or her sole responsibility.

National Library of Australia Cataloguing-in-Publication entry:

Edwards, Lyndal 2022 — LifeGardener: Seed, Plant & Grow Your Full Bloom Life

ISBN: 978-0-6455324-0-1

Edited by: Rowena Edwards and Lyndal Edwards

Author photograph: Lillian Reynolds – www.lilyreynoldsphotography.com

Cover art: Amanda McPaul – www.amandamcpaul.com.au

Illustrations: Tia Fereti – @belovedbuzz_art

Designed by Chávez & López Diseño Gráfico C.A.

For Olwyn, the grandmother
tree shading our family.

CONTENTS

INTRODUCTION	7
PART ONE: Illuminate	15
We are all LifeGardeners	23
You (almost always) reap what you sow	23
Death of the indoor plant	26
Presence brings power	27
Light changes everything	30
Ask the blooming questions	33
Seed your truest intentions	36
PART TWO: Enrich	43
Soil of your soul's desires	48
Dig deep for truth	50
What lies beneath: my job	52
What lies beneath: my daughter	53
Feed your dreams and desires	56
PART THREE: Cultivate	61
Stop controlling, start cultivating	66
Our Covid cultivation story	67
Cultivation is creative	68
Nature's ripening	69
Let it go, let it grow	71
Plant your way to power	72
Control freak confessional	74
Pack-drill holidays	74
Pre-party clean up	75
Cultivate body truth	77

PART FOUR: Flourish 83
Survive or thrive 89
Goddess in the garden 93
Dig deeper to self-nourish 94
Planting grace wasn't easy 95
Planting practical support 97
Self-centred living 98
Yin yang balance 99
Where's your sunshine? 102
Nourishing AM 103
Nourishing PM 104
Cultivating quiet time 105
Cultivating deep rest 108

PART FIVE: Grow 113
Seed the change 120
Compost your past to feed your future 122
Plant powerful intention seeds 126
Planting for growth 129
Harvest what grows 130
LifeGardening your way 132

PART SIX: Nurture 137
Nurture self-trust 144
Nurture some support 145
Nurture your time freedom 150
Nurture your authentic energy 151
Red hot energy 153
Nurture energetic intentions 154

PART SEVEN: Bloom	157
Cultivate your power	164
Plant organic goals	166
Harvesting the year that was	169
The LifeGardener Cultivation Cycle	171
LifeGardening by the seasons	172
Sharing your intentions and harvest	173
Shining the light – Goddess in the Garden	174
CONCLUSION	181
Epilogue	185
About the Author	189
Acknowledgements	190
Connect with the author	191
Download your free book bonuses	192

PROLOGUE

TRUTHSEED

n.

An idea or sense which, when held in your heart and mind, begins to germinate and calls to be planted deep in the soil of your life.

I recently planted a TruthSeed.

I don't want or need more of anything new.

I don't want to go higher or further, just deeper… have deeper relationships and more enriched experiences both within myself and in my life.

I know how to drive hard and fast to achieve just about anything, but I no longer want to be driven by others.

I don't feel a need to always 'shine', I just want to be more fully and freely the un-glossy, earthy me. And I know deep in the soil of my soul that whenever I allow myself to naturally, organically bloom – even just for a moment – so does my life.

I've come to realise my life is a garden, full of life, colour, fragrance and beauty. It's impacted by the weather – both my moods and my circumstances – and changes with the seasons.

There are times when I need to remove unwanted weeds in my work, relationships, or attitude, sift through what matters and compost the rest.

When I grew curious about this life-as-a-garden concept, a simple TruthSeed sprouted in my heart and mind: if my life really is a garden, and I consciously choose to be the Gardener, what might grow?

What would happen if I started to take responsibility for the persistent weeds? What if I began digging deeper into the soil beneath and looking at the quality of my choices and my life?

I began to cultivate a sense of curiosity for the deeper and richer layers of my life. What if, instead of trying to control situations and outcomes in my world, I began to cultivate and seed change and growth from inside myself?

What if, instead of doubting my decisions, I could trust myself, as the cultivator of my life, to take my natural next steps? What if I planted my actions from a place of authenticity, rooted in what matters to me?

What if I could compost my past to feed my future, turning hard-won lessons into fertile ground for self-love, self-growth and powerful change both within me and around me?

This book was seeded, planted and grown from that soil – an innate desire to savour the nectar of life's joys, plant powerful intention seeds and live my life with my feet not just firmly planted on the ground, but deeply rooted in what I know to be powerful and true.

What I know to be powerful and true is organic and continues to grow and strengthen its roots, as I am constantly blooming. I find freedom in this. Once upon a time, I saw a change of mind, or heart, or life direction as irresponsible and unreliable.

The wisdom of ageing has shown me my nature is as ever-changing and dynamic as nature and life itself. Personal evolution, the shedding, weeding and composting of our past to plant the natural next step and grow whatever is emerging, is wild, natural, and inevitable.

The blooming of ourselves and our life is beautiful and painful and deeply rich, especially if we choose to stay present to as much of it as we can bear at the time. As surely as the leaves colour and drop in autumn, we too drop and release what no longer serves us as a natural falling away.

Perhaps the most beautiful revelation is that the things my soul most longs for are profoundly simple and have remained unchanged my whole life.

In September 2021, while sifting and sorting the soil of my dreams, desires and longings, I – quite by accident, but with a heartfelt intention – unearthed seven of these SoulSeeds.

As I pulled into my driveway on a September Thursday morning, I asked myself, "In all this busyness and buzz of your life right now, in all the struggle you're feeling (once again) in your solar plexus and stiffened neck, what are you really longing for?"

My soul answered quickly, giving me just enough time to take notes:

"Hey, thanks for asking me instead of your head. Actually, my needs are simple. What I long for, what you have longed for all your adult life is: grace and ease (instead of stress and struggle); deeper relationships; to live with meaning and purpose; a deep and beautiful nature connection; a daily devotion to self-nourishment; strength of body and mind; and soulitude (alone time without the mind chatter)."

Surely there was more to it than this. These desires seemed too basic, too common, too unambitious. Then I real-eyesed. These aren't goals or projects to be seeded and planted, they are SoulSeeds crying out to be recognised as significant enough (as simple as they are), to be at the very centre of my LifeGarden.

In the days that followed, more SoulSeed insights fell onto my journal pages. This is the essence of what my soul asked of me:

- ❦ I want to live each day with grace and ease, to welcome the day, and for you to carry that grace and ease into as many present moments as you can.
- ❦ I want deeper, more heartfelt connections with those you love, taking the time to listen with your whole self and bringing a richness to each and every connection.
- ❦ I want you to live life with a richer meaning and purpose, releasing the pettiness and negativity, and showing up as your most powerful change-making self.
- ❦ I want you to lose and find yourself in deep nature connection, let nature heal and inspire you, and hunger to intimately know your wilder nature.
- ❦ I want you to listen well to what you need and desire, to your intuition as a guide to deeper truth, and to self-nourish as a devotion and practice
- ❦ I want you to build strength, of body and mind – so you can embrace your true power as a cultivator of powerful change in your life and the world.
- ❦ I want you to give yourself the soulitude you need to clear your mind and rejoice in your creativity, joy and inner Goddess.

I listened.

Listening saw me reject two busy work projects just weeks later.

Listening led me back to loving myself, those beautiful people around me – who'd been watching my recent work struggle – and those passion projects closest to my heart, including this book.

Listening helped me finish this book, to soften its heart, deepen its roots and bring the fragrance of truth and beauty I was longing to gift to you.

I am deeply grateful for these recent gifts and the generous, eternal blossoming of this simple life-as-a-garden metaphor.

I feel ripe and ready to share its power, magic and wisdom with you.

INTRODUCTION

LOCKDOWN BLOOM

My desire to write this book had been budding for years, but came into bloom in the spring of 2020, as we emerged from the first Covid-19 lockdown. Many things were lost or changed around the world during the global pandemic, including livelihoods and lives.

Everyone has a Covid-19 story to tell. My family's story is more fortunate than most. Our only real loss was control, and what grew inside me was confirmation that when nothing seems to be going to plan it's time to stop controlling and start cultivating.

As the Covid numbers and fear intensified around the world, I felt a strange liberation budding in my own heart and mind. Within this newfound time and space – quiet streets, cafes and highways – this life-as-a-garden idea was seeded and profoundly and irrevocably changed how I viewed, experienced and lived my life.

When the world seems to be tilting a little too far on its axis, and world leaders are polarising when they should be unifying, the natural reaction is to panic and tighten our grip. When we can't control what's happening 'out there', the temptation is to try to control what's going on 'in here' inside ourselves, our family and our community. What I noticed was the women around me were growing tired of holding on tight, of struggling for control of their lives.

Keeping all the balls in the air, juggling the demands of motherhood, of partnership, friendship and work is not only exhausting, it's distracting. When we're busy watching the balls in the air, there's no time or energy to see and give attention to the things that really matter in our heart, our soul, our world.

I hear so many women say they're frustrated and disheartened by the state of the world – social injustice, war, inequality, homelessness, environmental collapse – but they're so tired and so busy they don't know how to change the small corners of their own life, let alone contribute to positive change around them.

Perhaps you feel this in yourself, or witness it in others – a frustration and despair at the growing parts of life and the world that can't be controlled. LifeGardening offered me what I'm now offering you: seeds of hope and a fresh, new, organic way of cultivating powerful and positive change in yourself, your life and the world around you.

An invitation to garden

This book is an invitation to stop juggling, put down the balls and pick up the spade. Stop overthinking your life and dig your hands deep into its soil. Take a look at what lies beneath that top layer, for it holds the truth of your deepest dreams and desires, your passions, the things that lay dormant a while, then wake you at 3am to tug on your conscience.

Stop overthinking life's choices and start digging with passion and earnestness to uncover your own roots, your truth, and the passion with which to grow your one precious LifeGarden.

More than a philosophy for living, LifeGardener is a down-to-earth, get-your-hands-dirty guide to help you:

- **Illuminate Your Truth** – Shine the light of truth on what's really growing and showing in your life.

- **Self-Nourish to Flourish** - Discover new energy from your roots to your tips when you move beyond what you need to survive to what you know will help you thrive.

- **Seed Your Intentions** - Feel the power shift that comes when you stop over-thinking and plant your powerful intention seeds with simple actions.

- **Start Weeding** - Find ways to stop whingeing and start weeding what's no longer working in your life.

- **Compost Your Past** – Awaken to the fact that the past, no matter how toxic or weed-filled, can feed and fertilise your future dreams and desires.

- **Grow Organic Goals** – plant organic goals that grow and change as you do, blossoming beyond your imagination.

- **Cultivate Your Power** – learn to cultivate all the time, energy and support you need to seed, plant and grow your Full Bloom Life.

I'm both grateful and excited you've picked up this book. I hope we can journey together right until the end. I don't take your time and attention for granted and my daily devotion as I wrote the book was to you, dear reader.

I know this might feel a little too familiar early on, but I've been so committed to showing up at the writing desk and sharing with you that I feel much closer to you than you will to me right now.

Now this book is in your hands, or on your device, you can, of course, read it in whatever way feels right for you, flicking through parts to pick and harvest as you please. However, to experience the full bloom potential of the book, I would invite you to read from front to back for two reasons:

- From the moment I sat to write, the book grew and blossomed as effortlessly as a morning rose opens. The 40,000 plus word bounty grew in just six beautiful spring weeks in (almost) the exact order you are about to read it.

- Secondly, each part unearths a new layer of the LifeGardener philosophy. You'll notice exercises at the end of some parts. Each of these get-your-hands-dirty exercises has been planted with the intention of both awakening your consciousness and deepening your experience of LifeGardening.

You can see this book as an opportunity to 'stop and smell the roses' for a few hours, then pop it back on the shelf to collect dust. Or you can open your heart and mind to the potential blossoming of a new way of seeing yourself, living in and loving your life.

LifeGardening is 3 things

It's a philosophy for living and an empowering new way of seeing your life come into full bloom. But it's also a simple process – the LifeGardening Cultivation Cycle – for manifesting and cultivating everything from small, powerful changes to your biggest dreams and most heartfelt desires.

Thirdly, LifeGardening is a set of get-your-hands-dirty tools that you can use to practically cultivate positive and powerful changes in your life. I'll be sharing these – Intention Seeding, Action Planting, Grounded Visioning, Harvesting – throughout the book.

INTRODUCTION

There are a couple of basic gardening tools you'll be familiar with that will help you harvest your learnings. A journal or notepad of any kind and a pen is just about all you need.

My intention seeds

I want you to understand the very simple, yet deeply heartfelt intentions I am seeding in writing and sharing this book and powerful process with you.

- I want you to experience your power as the cultivator of your own life.

- I want to share TruthSeeds and ask you the blooming questions to grow and cultivate your curiosity.

- I want you to see, taste, smell and touch the divine nature of yourself and your LifeGarden.

- I want you to experience the freedom that begins to bloom when we seek and unearth self-truth, when we live our lives with our feet firmly planted in the soil of our soul's longing.

- I want you to tap into the root of true feminine power to create, to cultivate change, to bring your dreams and desires into bloom, and to help both yourself and those you love and care about flourish.

- And on a really practical level, I want you to feel the enjoyment that comes with living from a place of creative cultivation, rather than rigid control.

My promise to you is that I will be your LifeGardener guide, every step of the way. I will share with you my homegrown and handpicked ideas, tools and practices.

As your consciousness grows and you put these tools and techniques into practice, you'll discover what feels right for you. You'll find your own gardening style; you'll naturally cultivate the LifeGarden you love spending time in.

If you choose to embrace your life as a LifeGardener, as a conscious cultivator, you'll feel your inner power and confidence grow as your outer life comes into authentic full bloom. My hope is, you'll start to cultivate and grow your authentic, beautiful LifeGarden as naturally as the sun rises.

Are you ready? Let's begin.

Blooming with gratitude,

Lyndal

"What we seed, plant and consciously cultivate in our heart and mind creates the garden that is our life."

PART ONE
ILLUMINATE

INTENTION SEED

n.

Any one-off action, new habit or attitude shift you are considering planting in yourself and your life to grow positive change.

Olwyn died on my mother's birthday, 23 February 2016, with a full moon in her own sign, Virgo. Her hospital surroundings were far from ideal, but she died surrounded by love. From just two children of her own grew an abundant tribe of seven grandchildren and – at age 88 – 15 great grandchildren.

My nan's passing was one of the most profoundly beautiful memories of my life.

While she was conscious, she let me massage her feet with oil and lavender lotion. I'm not sure it gave her relief, but I loved the chance to connect with her in this simple and intimate way.

Truth be told, while she was conscious and I sat massaging her feet, I felt, somehow, she would pull through this and we'd go back to filling her champagne glass and topping up her prawn plate at Christmas. It was a well-known family fact that if you half-filled Olwyn's champagne glass she'd shoot you a look and ask, "Is there a drought?"

Her other insistence was for salt, which my partner Guy calls 'crack for old people'. If she had a dollar for every time she said, "pass the salt" she'd have died a wealthy woman indeed. Mum shared that Olwyn's last tiny meals in the hospital were in great need of salt and "Where's the salt?" was one of the last things nan managed to say.

When I returned to the foot of her bed after a break and she had lost consciousness, my instinct was to continue the massage ritual. Perhaps it was something she could feel even more now, without the distraction of room-filled conversation.

As I held her feet in my hands, a feeling of deep privilege washed over me. Solemnity swept through my body and being as I stroked her ankles and massaged oil and cream into the soles of her rough feet.

At the time of her fall, I'd been going through a dark, emotional tunnel and now, as she lay serenely, I felt her presence and reassurance stronger than ever before. Her spirit spoke gently to me: "Is this really what you want? Look after yourself."

In the moment it came through I didn't try to understand it. I just received her gentle, loving guidance. The resonance of her message stayed within me for the days and weeks that followed.

I returned home later that night and tried getting a little sleep, with plans to return to the hospital at first light. The large glass doors of my Blue Mountains bedroom verandah faced east towards the hospital down on the plains, Sydney's vast sea of lights beyond.

I was woken around 3am, the bright light of the full Virgo moon illuminating my yard, the verandah and my bedroom. The world seemed bathed in divine light. I reached for my phone and saw eight missed calls and messages.

My family had done all they could to reach me. I had accidentally left my phone on silent from the hospital and must have slept so heavily I wasn't woken by the vibrations.

I read the stream of messages, the final one simply, "she's gone". I dropped the phone, felt my heart bursting through my chest and stepped outside into the light. I wept for her ending, for my mother, for her whole beautiful tribe. Most of all I wept peacefully, still floating on the energy of her last message and the sacredness I felt at her feet.

I stepped back in from the moonlight and as I stared down towards the twinkling lights of the city below, a large owl landed on the balcony railing. It perched itself, turned its head a few times and flew away.

I was lifted by its presence, and assured her passing was perfectly peaceful. Despite the agony ahead for my darling mother and my family, this moment brought me nothing but peace. When I returned to the hospital to join my mum, her brother and my siblings, I knew this peace I felt was mine to hold quietly, for now.

When I returned to my car, I caught the last of the giant full moon setting over the Blue Mountains. A last divine goodbye. The grace of her filled me again.

When I say I was grateful for the experience of my nan's passing it's simply because I was as conscious as I was able to be throughout. Being in the presence of our family matriarch in the hours before she left this world felt nothing short of a divine privilege. As difficult as the experience was, I feel richer for it, for my willingness to stay present in all the sacred moments.

In this first part, I'll share how staying present and shining the light of truth on our experiences allows us to feel our way to what moves us deeply, what matters most. We'll uncover the innate power we carry inside – like an Olympic flame – to light our path through the darkness and consciously take our truest and most natural next step. And I'll share the TruthSeed that intention is everything. As actor and *Green Lights* author Matthew McConaughey put it, "Words are moments, intentions are momentous."

My hope is that Olwyn, my beautiful grandmother, knew the shade of her grace, beauty and generosity was and is enough for her whole abundant family. Like all who grew from her, I have much to be thankful for.

The gift of her death was that it reminded me of the richness of life. Not just in the clichéd *live life to the fullest* kind of way, although that's one of death's great lessons.

She showed me, as she slipped away, that we are all here to be as deeply present with each other as we humanly can be. Sitting with her as she died reminded me, we are human *beings*, not human *doings*.

It also reminded me that we each have the power to cultivate our own divine experience of life in each and every moment, each and every relationship, every single day.

If my nan's life were a garden, I imagine it began as a barren wasteland. Unloved and unwanted, her garden tells a familiar story of Depression life between the First and Second World Wars, when children were seen and not heard. On top of the generational pains, she had a rough, cruel start to life. I'm told her mother called her a 'dirty Jew'. Her skin and hair were darker and dirtier than her blonde princess sister.

I've had moments, while she was alive, when I was so deeply grateful to experience four generations of women of my lineage in one room. They say we stand on the shoulders of our ancestors, but the women in my family can stand on equal ground, knowing our mere presence and softness is enough to connect us to all that we are collectively cultivating – and that's a privilege.

As time passed, especially in her final years, she softened. Some could call this softening inevitable, given the glorious, abundant growth of her tribe. However, I believe some people choose to harden like an old tree as they age – not always consciously – and others go the other way. At some point she consciously chose to surrender to the sweetness and softness of our collective heart connection. It was a pleasure and an honour to witness.

She chose to start *smelling the roses*, she let love and light into her heart, including with my mother. In her final years, despite the physical irritations that come with ageing, her LifeGarden was a rambling estate, full of exotic delights, daphne, lilies and jasmine in bloom. I imagine her garden full of plants, surviving and thriving in places they shouldn't. And plenty of large trees with generous summer shade to cool her English self.

At the end of our life, all we have is memories. Those who practice being present can more easily recall the richness of those memories and draw on the intensely beautiful emotions of everyday minuscule moments. That's what I want.

I want a LifeGarden rooted in all the things I value most, nourishing the soil of my deepest and most authentic self. I know good things will grow in my life no matter what I do. But I want to look down on my LifeGarden – not just at my life's end, but every time I stop for a moment of gratitude – and see before and within me all the divine and incredible things I have planted, grown and cultivated.

When things get tough – and they will – I want to know my LifeGarden is so fragrant with love that even life's darkest moments will end, and I will grow and cultivate joy and love and laughter again.

I want to share in the fruits of my life's work, share the bounty of my abundant LifeGarden with those I love, and those who cannot yet see and feel their own ability to grow love in their garden.

I owe it to my grandmother, we owe it to all our grandmothers, to step beyond the darkness, struggle and limitations they have overcome. Whatever your grandmother's story, however she softened or hardened, you can consciously cultivate your own divine LifeGarden now, not wait until your final years.

Every single one of us is constantly cultivating our lives. Every choice we make, every action we take, every thought we germinate, influences what grows inside us and in our life.

You may not be aware of it, but you have some of your time and energy planting new ideas, weeding out unwanted habits and problems, composting your past and growing your goals, dreams and aspirations. You may not have been aware that LifeGardening is in your *nature*.

The only difference between you and I is that I have embraced the concept of being a LifeGardener, as a way of living life and making sense of what it is that I can cultivate in myself and my life, no matter how crazy and uncontrolled the world around me seems (and let's face it, then 2020s have given us plenty of crazy).

Consciously cultivating your life brings with it a responsibility. Stepping up as the gardener of your life can sound pretty daunting, particularly if you've been ignoring or neglecting some parts. It can seem like too big a job if some of your LifeGarden 'beds' feel completely overgrown with weeds. But it's the weeds that reveal the truth of what we could potentially release or weed and replant with the new.

We are all LifeGardeners

Being a LifeGardener is about making conscious choices that feed the soul, that bear positive fruit and make your LifeGarden a beautiful place to live in, for yourself and those you love. Every choice and decision is an opportunity to grow in strength, confidence and power, as the cultivator of your LifeGarden.

Like all things we learn, you can garden and grow at your own pace in your own way. The only prerequisite is the desire, the willingness, to start somewhere. The beautiful thing is, starting exactly where you are is just perfect.

You (almost always) reap what you sow

When you hear that expression, does it give you karmic shivers? Do you feel a burden of responsibility, as if everything you've experienced as bad, traumatic or stressful you somehow brought upon yourself?

Let me just set the record straight here and now. That kind of thinking is completely unhelpful. There are many terrible things that happen to good hearted, well intended people.

The LifeGardener version is this:

You reap what you sow, so try to be conscious of what you *want* to grow!

Although there's a level of responsibility inherent in this, there's also awesome potential for new growth, new beginnings, and self-determinism. Viewing your life as a garden and yourself as the LifeGardener means you have the power to plant something into a situation that could, potentially, completely change the outcome. This could be a simple action, a thought or belief, or words we say, or don't say, to another.

This concept bears fruit in both the short and long term. Here are some examples of seeding in the present moment:

- You're in an argument with someone you love, you're furious and they're pushing all your buttons. You feel your temperature rise and – just as you go to say something cutting – you stop yourself, breathe and say, "I just need a few minutes to cool down." New Action seed sown.

- You're running late for an appointment, speeding and stressing. You pull into a petrol station, call about your appointment and tell them you're late, buying yourself an extra 20 minutes. New Action seed sown.

- You're taking 30 minutes to sit down with a cuppa on the couch when one of your kids asks for some help with their homework. You're exhausted. You usually oblige, but this time you say, "Sweet, I'll join you at [insert time]. I'm just taking some quiet time." New Action seed sown.

Now, all of the above are present moment examples, but you can see how the smallest, sometimes split-second decisions, impact the quality of our experience. There's no guarantee any of the above actions will have a positive long-term impact. However, if we sow certain seeds often enough, the benefits will eventually grow. If we start regularly sowing the same kinds of seeds in similar situations, you can see how much more likely it is that you'll reap more positive outcomes.

What seed of change could you sow now?

Take a couple of minutes to consider the examples above. Is there a situation or regular conversation in your life that might call for a new seed of change to be sown? If you find one, try planting it next time the situation arises.

Here are some examples of longer-term sowing. Reality warning: these are real examples taken from my own life. (Let's start with the bad one first):

- Late 1988 - I'm about to head off on a Whitsundays holiday with my boyfriend's family. His parents are paying. I'm 19, working in their son's business and not drawing a wage. I am financially irresponsible, fiscally unconscious and hoping the debts I have accrued will magically disappear while I am on a vacation I do not deserve, filling my belly, buffet style, three times a day. In the last 72 hours before flying out, I receive calls from four different debtors chasing payments. I was reaping exactly what I had sown. I'd been sowing seeds of financial irresponsibility for years.

- Late 2017 - I step out on a Saturday night in December to perform at an annual African dancing and drumming concert known as *Banquet of Dreams*. I'm feeling and looking like a Goddess. I've been wanting to dance live for this amazing group (Hands, Heart and Feet) for years. The night has finally come. I step onto the dancefloor, nervous, treading on toes and apologising to other Goddesses around me. But I make it through. Not only that, I meet the man I'm going to marry. He's a part-time drummer. We agree to a date the next day and had seven dates in our first week. Yes, meeting Guy was magical, and yes, the outfit helped. But the fact is, I had spent the previous two years single, and not dating. Not only was I busy doing other things, but I had been sowing the seeds for a loving relationship and getting clear about what I was wanting to experience and was willing to bring. (More on this story in Part 5).

According to Albert Einstein, the definition of insanity is doing the same thing over and over and expecting a different result. The LifeGardener version is planting pineapples and expecting zucchinis.

I want you to take this notion – *You reap what you sow, so be conscious of what you grow* – with absolute lightness. I want to make this really clear: this book has grown from an organic desire to bring clarity, simplicity and freedom, not to burden or overwhelm.

When you're playing with each of the budding concepts in this book, take your time to explore and experience what's on offer, and you'll know what's ripe for your picking.

You can seed change in any given moment, simply by choosing to think, act or speak differently. Planting a new thought or action is how we plant and grow a better future in the present moment.

Once you awaken to this and become aware of its power, you can consciously cultivate big changes in small steps.

Death of the indoor plant

When I asked a green-thumbed friend of mine who gardens for a living, "What's the key to good gardening?" her answer was simple: observation. She suggested the best way to grow my food garden was to just start and then observe what happens along the way.

That wasn't really what I wanted to hear, although I knew it as truth. I had a 20-year long trail of short-lived and under-nourished indoor plants to remind myself of what life looks like when you're too busy to pay attention to the things that need food, water and sunshine.

I've come to realise my indoor plants are a direct reflection of the quality and richness of my life. Today – not to boast – my indoor beauties are thriving and onto their third repotting upgrade due to their unbridled lusciousness. This brings me more joy than my family can quite understand. Nevertheless, as I wipe dust from their thankful, deep green leaves and empty the last of my green tea into their eager pots, I smile widely both inside and out.

The state of my plants tells me I am awake and aware of my surroundings, paying attention and giving love where it's needed most, including to myself. I am no longer running through my life at great speed, missing the beautiful and important things. Covid-19 has made working from home a workable reality, and vastly increased the love and attention our indoor plants and pets have received. (Apparently, dogs are much happier about this than cats, who were much happier at home alone.)

Presence brings power

As you'll see from the pages ahead, I've spent much of my adult life like many women I know: too busy and time-poor for the little things that make a huge difference to the quality of my life and the richness and depth of my present moment experience.

Most tragically and importantly, being busy and not paying attention to what needs feeding and watering can bring a much higher penalty. Being too busy to slow down, get conscious and listen deeply to your heart and soul is the opposite of being deeply present, as present as I was at my grandmother's feet.

It's hard to stay conscious of life when you're super busy, and it's totally possible to be living your life and not actually be *in it* while it's playing out. It's the difference between watching live theatre and reading a theatre review. Not being present for the people you love means you miss the heartbeats between the words, the delicious moments of energetic bliss, elation, discomfort – the whole fruitful orchard of deep emotional connection.

Not being present can manifest in a number of ways. For me – and perhaps for you – it can look like this:

- I have to ask someone to repeat themselves because I wasn't listening, I was thinking about or distracted by something else.
- I start writing my mental shopping list or solving a problem in the middle of sex.
- I refuse to sit still long enough for my daughter to speak to me, instead asking her to follow me around the house because I'm busy with something else that can't wait.
- I get fidgety during a boring work video call, turn off the camera and start on something else.
- When I'm interrupted by a phone call or someone walking in while I'm in the middle of something, I feel my neck tighten, sigh audibly and want the conversation to be over before it's begun.
- When listening to someone speak, I butt in with my opinion before they have a chance to get the last word out.
- I see every little unexpected interruption of my 'flow' as an annoyance, rather than accepting what's happening in the present moment.
- I feel a general sense of unease, like wherever I am and whatever I'm doing, I should be somewhere else doing something else.
- I start to feel fragmented in my mind, like a mosaic waiting to be made, bits of broken tiles lying everywhere with nothing 'coming together'. (This feeling is quite common when I've been over-scrolling on social media or jumping from one thing to another for too long).

♣ I feel anxious and in need of space and time to myself, get snappy and short tempered with everything and everyone. (This is a sure sign I haven't been present enough to create spaciousness within and between the things I've been doing and the conversations I've been having).

In my experience the most devastating periods of non-consciousness have come from not being present with myself, my inner knowing, my self-truth. My ability to move through life while ignoring what my gut instinct was saying, sometimes screaming, still blows my mind when I look back.

When I reflect on the abusive bosses I endured and the long-dead relationships I over-stayed, I realise it's completely possible for a sane, seemingly happy and healthy human to function on the surface while ignoring the truth that lies beneath in the deep, rich soil of her soul's longing.

I know this because I *did* this, repeatedly.

What my green thumb friend told me to do with my food garden – plant then observe what happens – sounded like work to me, and all I wanted was a simple and bountiful food garden I could chart, plant, harvest and rotate on my (Virgo inspired) gardening planner. What I've come to realise in my life is that there is no set-and-forget, plant and walk away.

Life's garden does not grow according to our plans, our planting charts. And sometimes, when we look closely at what's been growing – in our life, relationships, in ourselves – while we weren't paying attention, it's deeply painful to look at. For me, when I've looked long and deep at the most weed-infested parts of my life, my biggest and toughest weeds were the things I hadn't done, the decisions I hadn't made and had left for others to make *for me*.

The weediest of my LifeGarden beds have been in the areas of money and intimate relationships. How did I manage to get through the 'weed watching' without falling into a pit of deep shame and despair? I dug deep and tapped into the deeply rooted, deliberately hidden moments and memories in search of clarity and freedom.

I did what I've now termed *Compost My Past to Feed My Future*. I'll share a little of it in this part, then dive more deeply into the intimate process as we get to know each other a little better.

Down there, in the depths and darkness of self-truth – digging through the past of my relationships and finances in order to make better, healthier and more informed choices – I never really felt alone, because I took the light with me.

Light changes everything

When you travel into a dark cave with a head torch or down a hallway with a candle, your intention isn't to keep the dark away, it's to light the path right in front of you so you can take your next step with just enough confidence and courage. You can never see the whole darkness, that's the point. Your only task is to take one step at a time.

The same applies to our past, our self-truth. You never really know until you venture into your own darkness what might appear. Even if you've walked this very same cave or hallway several times before, there's every chance you could be surprised by what you find, feel, encounter and unearth.

What do you carry with you when you're afraid of the dark of your past? Some people carry faith, others hope or prayer. In my recent experiences into the darkness of relationship and money past, I've been led by two sources of light. The first is my very clear and heartfelt double intention:

- to dig deep into the soil of my past to uncover my self-truth, no matter how raw or scary.
- to uproot the fear and shame, then shine the light of self-compassion so my soul can continue to grow and bloom toward the light of its own truth.

Self-compassion is vital. It's the key here. Without self-compassion there is shame. Without self-compassion there is self-judgement. Without self-compassion there is paralysis. Self-compassion is the cradle that gently rocks the mind, body and spirit as it journeys through the painful process of growth and evolution.

The second light source I call on to guide me through the darkness on my quest for self-truth is divinity. God, the source, guides, grandmothers, angels, Buddha, Gaia. It matters far less to me what we call our connection to the divine than that we can choose to be connected and supported at any moment.

On a recent early morning beach walk a woman approached me. She seemed both blissful and bursting with enthusiasm. I smiled at her. "This is my church," she said, pointing to the quiet, soft silken sea and morning light. "It's a sacred time of the day," I answered. We spoke for a short time, but our conversation went deep.

When it ended and she hopped into her car, she paused and called out to thank me for our rich and deep conversation. I came away with a familiar buzz, not an ego or adrenal buzz, but a steady, content vibration that reminded me how it feels to speak openly and bravely. This is how it is when two humans see, hear and feel each other fully, when souls dance together freely and effortlessly; no agenda, no past, no future, just pure connection in the moment.

For me, this vibration is my reminder of what it feels like to be heard, seen, safe, supported, connected, and loved. Not just by another, but by life and the universe. So, when I dive bravely and deeply into my past or a situation so I can *Compost my Past to Feed my Future,* I consciously and clearly ask for universal support.

I say or write "Thank you Universe for what you are about to show me, and for supporting and guiding me to truth." Sometimes I'll ask for my highest truth. I know when I ask for the universe to Illuminate, to *Shine to Light of Truth*, I cannot control what that means. I have no idea what will be uncovered, how painful it may be. I simply trust that it's essential to my growth, and that, if I walk with the light of self-compassion and universal divine support, I will be safely cradled.

Why would anyone even bother putting themselves through the potential pain of diving into the deep soil of the past? Why not just plant something new in your life and move on?

If you've ever had a garden, you'll know how persistent weeds can be, and how satisfying it is to remove them and give other things a chance to grow. Only you know if one or more of the beds in your LifeGarden needs weeding. I don't need to point it out to you. You know what needs attending to, what's lacking water and growing the most weeds.

Where are your weeds?

Without any sense of judgement and with as much self-compassion as you can muster, what does your instinct tell you about where the weeds are in your life right now?

When trying to make positive change in any area of your LifeGarden, you need to start exactly where you are, with self-truth. If there's an area of your life you've neglected, it may need some serious feeding, watering and nurturing to bring it back to life.

But the starting point is always Illumination. I usually start by just asking myself, like a friend would ask, what's going on in this area of my life. Sometimes the questioning is prompted by a gut feeling that I need to give something or someone some nurturing and attention. Other times, it comes from a conversation, or argument that reveals just how deeply rooted a problem is.

One thing I've come to know is the deeper you dig for the truth, and the more you Illuminate the truth of where you've been and who you're becoming, the more beautiful and fragrant the blossoming of you.

Ask the blooming questions

I've learnt to go easy on myself when seeking truth. It can be hard to hear and see what you've let grow inside yourself and your life. I've come to understand that shame is not helpful, and that the softness that comes from allowing yourself to gently open like a flower to the truth of any situation requires understanding and forgiveness.

As I dig deeper into the soil of my truth, I do so from a place of gentle self-curiosity, not blame or interrogation. In my experience, the more loving and kind I am with the Blooming Questions I ask myself, the more likely it is that the whole-hearted, fully fragrant truth will reveal itself.

The questions are often more important and powerful than the answers. When the questions you ask yourself – when you write them down or ponder them – elicit a response from deep within your body, you're probably tapping the roots of truth. Even the slightest feeling, tingle or discomfort can reveal signs of shift and change – potential transformation – even before you try to answer the question.

Starting simple, there are three questions I use to dig into the truth of what's going on in a particular area of my life:

- What is going on, really?
- How is it impacting me and others?
- How do I feel about it?

I'm big on journaling, so I find freewriting useful. Sometimes it's emotionally charged at first, sometimes I draw a blank but, eventually, the picture starts to emerge. (If you want to try answering these questions, there's an exercise at the end of this part).

I have a *soul sister*, Alison. We frequently leave WhatsApp messages for each other, talking through whatever's going on in our lives, big and small. I noticed that when she left a series of messages, she often resolved her issues while talking. She'd dig deeper and deeper with each message. The final message would often be, "Thanks for listening, I feel so much better now."

For a while, when either of us would do this, we would apologise for ranting or rambling on. One day I suggested to her we should find a more positive term for it, as it was working well for both of us to talk out loud without interruption. We decided on *Wandering*. If you don't have someone you can WhatsApp Wander with, you can always use your voice recorder on your phone.

My favourite kind of Wandering is in nature. I've loved walking for as long as I can remember. The miracle of walking out your thoughts and issues is you almost always arrive in a much clearer, stronger, wiser state. I don't think I've ever stormed out of a conversation, taken a walk and come back angry. Equally, I've never left the house with stress or a problem and not returned a little freer and closer to a solution. Nature's magical that way.

The second question is a useful one: "How is this impacting me and others?" Sometimes something that bugs or irritates us has zero impact on those around us. The issue wouldn't be tugging at you if you didn't think it needed attention.

The third question, "How do I feel about it?" can be huge! My strongest example of this is around money. When I first started cultivating my money garden, illuminating my feelings around the issue shone the light of truth on a lifetime of lies, self-deception and irresponsibility. It took me all the way back to my childhood when the lights would unexpectedly go out because Mum and (step) Dad hadn't paid the electricity bill.

I went back to seeing mum at the grocery store, after she realised she'd picked up more food than we could afford, giving the yummiest foods back to the checkout girl. There was a looooong list of seeds that were planted in these first (almost 50) years of my life before I began cultivating a more positive and powerful money LifeGarden. (More on that in Part 5).

When we first open our eyes to what's going on in certain areas of our life, on the surface, things can seem clear and simple. But when we start to look closer, dig deeper, and illuminate truth, that's when things get powerful.

All that digging down deep to illuminate your unique truth and the root causes enriches the soil for you to plant your next potential steps – your Intention Seeds.

Seed your truest intentions

Imagine for a moment that every seed in the world looked the same on the outside, and that the only way you could determine what you grew was by having a clear and powerful intention. If you intended on growing apples, you'd grow apples; if you intended on growing tomatoes, you'd grow tomatoes. You simply had to be clear about what you wanted and that's what you'd get.

Imagine now that every seed in the world still looked the same on the outside, but no matter how much you thought about it or tried to will apples into growing, you had no control over what grew from that seed. You'd have to be happy with whatever you got. "You get what you get, and you don't get upset."

This is a great metaphor for life, right? Sometimes we feel we can *will* things into growing our way. Other times, we've got no idea what's the hell's going on or how we got here!

In LifeGardener language, an Intention Seed is any new Action, Habit or Attitude shift you're considering planting into your life. For example, in the case of money, that could mean:

- Paying bills on time – Habit Intention Seed
- Spending thirty minutes on Monday nights talking money with your partner – Habit Intention Seed
- Saving 10% of your weekly wage – Habit Intention Seed
- Creating a new money mantra each week – Attitude Intention Seed
- Finding a money mentor or book with great reviews – Action Intention Seed

The LifeGardener way is to understand that if you're going to plant something, you'd better be sure you want it to grow (What you reap is what you sow).

Intention Seeds take this notion two powerful steps further:

Step 1 – Stay open to your Intention Seed's Potential
Don't tell your seed what it's going to grow into. If the weather's too wet, too dry or too windy, your Intention Seed may not make it. Certain things in our life only grow in just the right conditions. And there's a more beautiful reason to avoid limiting your Intention Seed's potential: what grows from your Intention Seed – whether it's a simple action, habit, or attitude – may be wildly *better* than what you planned (planted) in the first place.

Step 2 – Plant your Intention Seeds in rich soil
The more you practice digging into your truth, the more powerful the potential is for your Intention Seeds to grow. They will grow from a place of authenticity and truth, rather than growing from someone else's expectations or agenda. And as your negative patterns, actions and beliefs show themselves – as they will – you can use these as compost to enrich your desires for change and feed your future. (More on *composting* in Part Four).

Here are some simple questions I ask myself when looking to create new Intention Seeds in an area of my LifeGarden:

- What do I want to change (within and around me)?
- What am I willing and wanting to do to make this change happen?
- What is one thing I could take action on now?

Unlike the Illumination process, which digs down deep, I tend to just go with my intuition and keep this fairly light. Sometimes I prefer to do some visual journaling (doodling and drawing) rather than just writing. I draw little seed shapes and write around them and keep my mind open to all sorts of possibilities. The more open and relaxed your mind is – like a light warm breeze – the easier this part seems to flow.

There's no right or wrong. And remember, these are just *Intention Seeds*. This is just a written exercise, a bit of exploration, like wandering with appreciation through your favourite garden. You haven't committed to actually planting anything. We've got the whole book to explore planting, seeding, weeding, composting and cultivating together.

PART ONE: ILLUMINATE

LifeGardening Exercise

---◆---

ILLUMINATE + SEED

Ready to get your hands dirty?

Pick just one area of your life – money, job, career, relationships, parenthood, creativity, self-care, health, family, friendships, community work, a project… anything.

STEP 1

Illumination

Grab a journal or piece of paper and pen to explore the following questions:

- What is going on, really?
- How is it influencing or impacting my life and relationship with others in positive and negative ways?
- How do I feel about it?

If you need more time to dig deep on this one, consider taking a walk in nature, talking this through with a friend, or recording your voice on your smartphone.

STEP 2
INTENTION SEEDING

Now that you feel you've Illuminated what's true for you in this area of your life, explore (with lightness) the following questions.

Remember, you're looking to explore what Intention Seeds – actions, habits, attitudes – you could possibly plant to seed change:

- What do I want to change (within and around me)?
- What am I willing and wanting to do to make this change happen? (write 3-5 ideas)
- What is one thing I could take action on now?

Now do that thing, plant that seed, and feel your cultivation powers grow!

Part One Harvest

Let's recap what's been Illuminated in Part One:

- **We are all LifeGardeners.** You may not be aware of it, but you have spent time and energy planting new ideas, weeding out unwanted habits and problems, composting your past and growing your goals, dreams and aspirations. You just may not be aware of it.

- **You reap what you sow.** You can seed change in any given moment, simply by choosing to think, act or speak differently. Planting a new thought or action is how we 'seed' our future, how we create a better future in the present moment.

- **Light changes everything.** The deeper you dig for truth, the more you Illuminate where you've been and who you are becoming, and the more beautiful and fragrant the blossoming of you.

- **Ask the Blooming Questions.** When the questions you ask yourself elicit a response from deep within your body, you're probably tapping the roots of truth. Even the slightest feeling, tingle or discomfort can reveal signs of shift and change, even before you answer the questions.

- **Seed your truest Intentions.** Explore the Intentions Seeds – the actions, new habits or attitude shifts – you could plant in yourself or your life, to cultivate positive change.

> "Rather than love, than money, than fame, give me truth."
>
> Henry David Thoreau

PART TWO

ENRICH

SEEDCHRONICITY

n.

The moment when an idea, wish or intention you planted in the soil of your heart and mind meets the perfect conditions, and comes into blooming reality.

The day after I finished writing the LifeGardening Exercise in Part one, a miracle happened. I call these timely miracles and coincidences Seedchronicities. The first conversation of the day with my partner Guy, triggered an intense argument that brought up the single biggest stress point in our family, the one we had been avoiding discussing and which was slowly but surely eating away at the heart of our relationship. I bravely asked his permission to work through the exercise I'd written about the day before.

We began with the Illumination process, asking Blooming Questions:

What is really going on?

How is it influencing or impacting our life and relationship in positive and negative ways?

How do we feel about it?

Given the intensity of the subject I won't reveal details, in respecting my daughter's privacy. I feel it's worth sharing this process as it could be applied to many types of problems or situations.

For us, this step in the Illumination process was emotionally momentous, as if we were slicing the top off a volcano and allowing all that built-up hot, molten lava to work its way out into the light of day. We had never, in our three years together, given each other permission to pour out all our fears, anxieties and ancient wounds around this subject. And for the first time, we not only released all the tension, but we listened deeply.

This wasn't easy. It was uncomfortable, unfamiliar, and hard to speak to and listen to at times. But we both knew this was important and beautiful work.

I created this Illumination exercise for LifeGardeners to take a close look at what's impacting them and accept whatever feelings may arise, to illuminate their authentic truth.

What I hadn't considered until that moment is how powerful this part of the process could be with two people – a couple, a parent and child, friends, or family. For us, the shift in our understanding of each other was instant and profound. With tears and vulnerability came deeper truths. It became clear to us that we needed to take responsibility for composting our issues, so we didn't drag the weight of them through the process with our girl.

We both consciously acknowledged, out loud, what our deepest fears and anxieties were, so we could shine light on them – Illuminating our authentic truth, bearing witness for each other.

This Illumination deepened and powered up the next steps in the process, particularly when it came to asking, "What do I want to change (within and around me)?"

If we had skipped the Illumination questions and gone straight into this question, I guarantee we'd have been coming up with all the ways our daughter needed to change, all the things we could show and teach her in order to *fix her* problem, all the ways we could step in and 'save the day' as her parents.

Thank the Garden Goddess we didn't! Because the light of truth was clearly illuminating that it was *our* attitudes that needed to shift most of all. Yes, we wanted things to be better for her, but we realised whatever Intention Seeds we were planting, were for all of us to grow and change, not just her.

We ended up with a bounty of Intention Seeds – we could potentially plant into action - and we picked just a few to act on straight away.

Acting on something that's bothering you is great. But when that action, habit or attitude has been created as an Intention Seed, from a place of Illuminated truth and authenticity, it has an inherent potency. Any Intention created in light, instead of out of fear and desperation, is powerful and contains both the essence of authentic Intention and limitless potential for growth. (More on how to create powerful Intention Seeds in Part four).

The most divine part of this whole process was that the emotional eruption and vulnerability allowed for a softness to bloom between us and within us. (So often when I'm just *getting on with it,* making stuff happen, taking action, there's a hardness that comes with it).

Creating Intentions from our tears allowed us to stay in our heartspace, to maintain that softness of being, rather than the hardness of doing. Softness allows us to stay open like a flower, and to break through the clouds of the typically limited mind.

In this part, I want to share with you the value of being present with yourself and others to hold space for what arises when you choose to dig deeply with heartfelt intention. We'll start to explore some simple processes for digging into the soil of your own truth and see how this can help feed and fertilise your deepest dreams and desires.

When Guy and I finished our Illumination and Intention Seeding process, we sat quietly with our eyes closed and spent a few minutes letting ourselves daydream and Vision. Then we shared what we had seen and felt. We had so much love, truth and power in and around us that we could see through our heart's eye what we wanted our daughter to experience. We could see and feel and embody all the possibilities, all the potential that lay within the Intention Seeds we had just created together.

Cultivating a Vision – or Grounded Visioning in LifeGardener terms – is something I frequently do in my personal life and work. (I'll share more about the Grounded Visioning process in Part five). This was the first time Guy and I Visioned together. He was deeply moved by the process. He said it gave him something to 'see', to return to as a reminder of what we were both hoping for. When it came to having my first conversation with my daughter, I began first with a powerful intention – to listen deeply and to talk little (two ears, one mouth).

Even before the conversation began, I saw her in a different light, because my Intention had changed, my Vision of what was possible was so beautiful, and I realised it would be of her own unique creation. All I had to ask was, "What can we do to support you?"

I wanted to share with you the experience that came from working through this powerful process. Now I want to take Part one's learnings and help you dig much deeper into your own rich soil, starting to fertilise your dreams and desires.

Soil of your soul's desires

A seed is just a seed. It won't grow unless you plant it. And the quality of the soil you plant your precious seeds in will determine whether it withers or takes root and flourishes.

The same goes for our own actions. Can you recall a time when you tried and tried to make something happen, you took the actions you thought you needed to take, but whatever it was you were trying to force just didn't take root?

Some people would say it just wasn't meant to be. Some might say you just didn't try hard enough... try and try again. For me, it falls somewhere in the middle. I believe there are some things you just have to get through, and these things can be tough. I think of those as the endurance events in my life.

But for the most part, when things I'm trying to do just don't take root, it's because of one of these reasons:

- **It's not the season** – either I'm not ready or that thing isn't ready. Once upon a time, I pushed hard against this. But the more open I am about the possibility that all things have a ripe time to bloom and fruit, in myself and the world, the more organic and easy my life feels.

- **My intentions weren't true** – trying to make this thing happen had nothing to do with clear, true intentions. Perhaps I felt I should seed this, because of someone else's agenda or needs. Perhaps I was planting *their* Intention Seed in my own garden.

- **My soil wasn't fertile** – I came up will a great idea, which was well intended but simply wasn't aligned with anything I value. I typically do this when I find a thing to do that makes sense, might even be fruitful and helpful to someone else, but it's just not rooted in my values, dreams and desires. This is one of the ways, for years, I procrastinated on my own dreams and desires, blaming the pressures of motherhood, work and all I had to do for everyone else.

Think of the soil in your LifeGarden as holding your heart and soul's desires. It's rich with your truest motivations, it's what feeds and nourishes your actions, and it gives them the greatest chance to thrive. Of course, the more we experience in our lives, the clearer we become about what our values are rooted in, what matters most, and what we dream and desire to bloom in and around us.

Some of these life lessons are hard won, and some of our most painful experiences and endurance events Illuminate what we *don't* want to experience and have growing in our lives. Just as the key to gardening is observation, so the key to good LifeGardening is observing what's happening and illuminating the truth of what you've learnt along the way.

As we ripen in our years, our wisdom brings great fruit. If we're willing to stay conscious we can allow that wisdom to help us make the choices about what we let grow, what we weed, what we compost — what we cultivate next.

When we stop for a while and take a look at our lives, if things aren't growing and showing in alignment with our values, dreams and desires, it could be that something's not quite right in the soil beneath.

Dig deep for truth

Have you ever looked at someone's life — and I don't mean their Insta or Facebook life — and had this overwhelming sense that they were living their most authentic, joyful, full bloom life? It might be the way they spoke with clarity and passion, full-body laughed, or just how healthy and happy they seemed.

Did it make you envious or did it make you feel inspired to seek that same contentment? When we see people living their lives in this way it's easy to feel jealous and hope there's some secret big darkness in their relationship or something negative lurking in their lives.

I think we're so used to seeing positive versions of people's lives on social media that when we see a healthy, happy life offline, we're sceptical. It's understandable. But in my experience, what's growing and showing in someone's real life often says a lot about what lies beneath – in their soil.

If a person seems genuinely content with their lot in life, they're often walking the talk. Not *livin' the dream,* but literally living their unique dreams, the ones they've created, nurtured and cultivated.

If we stay conscious as we observe other people, other couples, other families, other professionals, and we notice not just how they are living but how *we react* to the way they are living, we can learn a lot about what matters most to us and what we want more or less of in our own lives.

Whenever I see someone travelling light, living simply and having an adventure, I'm reminded I really don't need much *stuff* to live, I'm an adventurer at heart, and getting off the treadmill sometimes, to wander through my day or weekend is good for my soul.

Whenever I see a woman doing yoga out in nature (even in a magazine), I feel instantly connected to my body. I want to rip off my shoes, feel the earth beneath my feet and salute the sun. It reminds me that time alone, especially in nature, does wonders to nourish my body and being.

When I saw couples kissing in public and holding hands, it used to remind me of what I didn't have in my relationship. But it also helped me plant the seeds of possibility for a romantic, expressive love relationship in the future, which is now in full bloom in my present.

Staying conscious of the feelings that arise and staying awake through the tough moments in our lives nourishes the rich soil that will feed our future dreams and desires.

When you look at what's growing and showing in your own life, it can reveal a lot about what lies beneath, what's feeding the growth.

Let me share with you some of what's growing and showing in two areas of my life, and the values and beliefs that lie beneath, in the soil, at this moment.

What lies beneath: my job

At the time of writing, I have a full-time job that can be highly stressful. My role is about helping people in community who are experiencing a threat or situation that is currently impacting, or may one day impact, them or their lifestyle to a significant extent. I'm paid by organisations to create a bridge between the people affected (community) and the corporation or government organisation (client).

I see my role as a diplomat, a peace-keeper, a problem solver and, most of all, to bring peace-of-mind through a challenging process. At times, it's a tough role, but I bring all the clarity, humanity and respect I can to it. It's not my dream job, but it's helped make some of my biggest dreams come true.

My dream job is doing what I'm doing at this very moment: writing and sharing in my most authentic and heartfelt way, connecting with you on the page. So why, apart from the money, do I choose to do a highly stressful job? Because it allows me to work from some of my deepest values:

- Clear communication – I cut through the corporate speak
- Optimism – I look for better outcomes
- Authenticity – If I can't help solve the problem, I don't bullshit

- Respect – If I promise something, I follow through
- Teamwork – I support whenever I can
- Peace-of-mind – I do what I can to help people sleep at night

These are just some of the work values that drive me to get up and open that laptop, switch on the phone, and face the day, even when I know it might be a tough one. These values have grown from years in crappy jobs with awful bosses, being paid to do and say things I didn't want to.

What lies beneath: my daughter

My teenage daughter Lily, at the age of seventeen, moved out of home. After scanning the local available living options, we landed on two. One was a divine granny flat cottage surrounded by gorgeous gardens. The main house was empty during the week, though the downstairs was rented by two yoga teachers – perfect for my non-partying teen.

The second, for the same price, was an immaculate share accommodation option in a two-bedroom granny flat with a large pool and deck. It was walking distance to everything – school, gym, friends, shops and potential jobs. Option two would mean less train trips (she didn't drive yet), and she'd be hugely popular with a pool!

We viewed both in the same day and on the drive back, she was really struggling. We'd talked through all the pros and cons. Option two was the clear leader, with all the mod cons and a fully stocked, ready to go kitchen plus an internal laundry. (Both houses had previously been listed with Airbnb and were fully furnished).

At some point in the conversation, she shifted from her head to her heart, dropping in and connecting to her authentic truth. She talked about seeing herself living in each place and said she'd clearly be happier living alone in the cottage. She turned to me and said, 'Mum, I know it's not as perfect as the other, but I don't need perfect, I'm seventeen. What I want most of all is to make my own decisions about what I do, when I do it, how loud I sing, who I have over.'

She added, 'This may be my last chance to ever live alone, and I really want that.' I told her how incredibly proud I was of her, that she was honest with herself about what really mattered to her. What she truly valued more than anything was freedom and autonomy.

It's important to remember that life is organic, dynamic. What's of value to us now may change over time or may deepen through rich experience. When she spoke her truth, Lily made it clear that not only was she aware of what mattered to her right now, but that she wanted to honour and follow that desire while it was still within her.

I bowed down to her wisdom, at seventeen. Later that evening when I shared the conversation with my mother, she asked if I wished I'd been that conscious at her age and made different decisions. *Hell yes!*

PART TWO: ENRICH

◆

What's growing in you?

For this next section, grab a paper or journal and pen.

Let's wander around your garden together and see what's growing and showing in your life. Draw circles on your page and label them with different areas of your life: money, work, relationships, creative projects, hobbies, health, etc. I like to call these garden beds.

Take a few minutes to jot down what it is you see happening – growing – in each area of your life. If a strong emotion comes up for a specific area of your life, write it down while it's fresh.

It doesn't matter whether what you see is something you have consciously grown or something that's grown on its own. If you notice any weeds growing, things you'd prefer weren't there, make a weed note, or draw one in and label it *weed*.

When you've finished this part of the exercise, take a minute or two to look at what you've harvested. What feelings arise when you look at your life as a whole garden? Write those feelings down. There is no right or wrong. This simple task is your first powerful step to becoming a LifeGardener.

You have Illuminated your own Life Garden. You have taken the first steps to shining the light of truth on your life as it grows, right now. Thank you for your willingness to start this process, to take your first barefoot, authentic step towards cultivating your own full bloom life.

Feed your dreams and desires

Have you ever dug your hands deep into rich soil and turned it over, the scent of sensual earth entering your nostrils, awakening every cell in your body? Have you lifted food straight from the earth, shaken it free from soil and eaten it fresh?

Have you ever, in the middle of a normal day, had the goosebump realisation that one of your biggest dreams is coming to life – that you have grown it and are living it? Have you ever realised that the ache you were carrying for your desire to manifest has been replaced by joy and elation because it's happening right in front of and within you?

I can tell you from experience that, when you wake up and realise you are living a life you have dreamed of, reaping the harvest of desires you have consciously cultivated, you will experience the full meaning of personal growth and (full body goosebump) empowerment.

You have the power to grow your heart's desires. You have the power to cultivate deeper relationships, more meaningful connections, work that lights you up, a home life that feeds and nourishes your soul, rituals that ground and centre you, a lifestyle that reflects all that you value and desire. All of these things are possible, one small but powerful planting at a time.

If you believe this to be true but aren't quite sure why your dreams have stayed dreams and not become your reality, then it might be time to start with your soil. Make a commitment, today, to start to feed and fertilise your desires.

Now that I've seeded this idea – the commitment to feed and fertilise your desires – I'll remind you throughout this book to return to your own authentic soil, to dig deep and pay attention to what lies beneath. Let's do a little of that now.

LifeGardening Exercise

WHAT LIES BENEATH?

Let's take your 'What's Growing and Showing' insights and dig deeper a little deeper.

STEP 1

What's growing that you love?

Grab your LifeGardener garden bed drawing from earlier and find an area of your life that you are happy or satisfied with. Expand on what you've already written or drawn by writing more about what's growing and showing. Write until you feel done.

Then, ask yourself the following questions:

- What is it about this area of my life that makes me feel good?
- How does it reflect what matters most to me – my values and beliefs?
- What would my greatest desire or biggest dream be for this area of my life?

STEP 2

What's growing the most weeds?

Find an area of your life you feel the least satisfied with, like you have little control, or it's overgrown with 'weeds'. It might be something you've been neglecting or ignoring. Expand on what you've written or drawn by writing more about what's growing or showing. Try not to judge yourself, others or the situation. Write until you feel done.

Then ask yourself the following questions:

- How do I feel about this area of my life?
- How does the situation reflect what I do and don't want in my life?
- Now that I've looked at this more closely, what could this part of my life look like if it reflected what I want and desire?

Part Two Harvest

Let's recap what we've dug deep on in Part Two:

- ❧ **Your soil is the soul of your LifeGarden.** It holds your heart and soul's desires. It's rich with your truest motivations, it's what feeds and nourishes your actions and gives your Intention Seeds the greatest chance to thrive.

- ❧ **Dig deep into your rich soil.** When you take a look at what's growing and showing in your own life, it can reveal a lot about what lies beneath, what's feeding the growth.

- ❧ **You're getting your hands (and feet) dirty. You're amazing!** Thank you for your willingness to start this process, to take your first barefoot, authentic step towards cultivating your own full bloom life.

- ❧ **Feed and fertilise your dreams and desires.** You have the power to grow your heart's desires. When you wake up and realise you are living a life you have dreamed of or reaping and harvesting the desires and outcomes you have consciously cultivated, you will experience the true meaning of personal growth and empowerment.

"The soul walks not upon a line,
neither does it grow like a reed.
The soul unfolds itself,
like a lotus of countless petals."

Kahlil Gibran, The Prophet

PART THREE
CULTIVATE

CULTIVATE

v.

To consciously create your future by choosing what to seed, plant and grow in your mind and in your life.

Eleven year-old Amy sat in the passenger seat on our drive to school. "The sun's so bright," she said, and I automatically leant across to pull down her visor. "Stop, mum!' she yelled, her hand firm on the visor. "I don't need it down."

I'd completely forgotten that just the day before, while travelling with Guy, she'd pulled down her visor to find a large hairy spider, and slammed it shut again, screaming. I apologised.

"You know what, mum," she began, "I've noticed lately you've been doing a whole lot of stuff I haven't asked you to do, without permission. Like last night when I told you I made a mistake on my project and you opened the liquid paper and leaned across to correct it.

"And how the day before," (there was more), "when we were out shopping for your birthday present, you picked it out yourself and told me it was from me," she said.

It was embarrassing and hard to hear, but I knew it as truth because I'd been observing these things in recent days and was surprising even myself. She added, "I'm finding it kind of annoying, but really sweet too, because I know you're trying to help."

I asked her to keep talking. She lightened the conversation, as she does. "Mum, imagine you've turned up to a party with the best wine and chips. They open the door and say, 'Hi, nice wine and chips... but you weren't invited.'"

Then, she floored me with, "Mum, you have to find a way to stop doing it so Lily and I can grow up and become the women we need to become."

In this part, I'm going to share some of the ways I've let my need to control steal the joy from my life and those I love the most. I'll Illuminate some of the ways controlling can worm its way into your LifeGarden and threaten the blossoming of things and people that matter most to you.

It was only a short time after that exchange in the car that I realised Amy wasn't my only victim. My eldest daughter Lily, (seventeen at the time), had recently moved back in with us after her eight-week stint living in the granny flat during a Covid-19 lockdown (so she could return to face-to-face schooling). I couldn't help but notice she had to ask me every time she was cutting vegetables for dinner, which way to do it. When I questioned her, she said, "When I'm by myself it doesn't matter, but back here with you I want to get it right."

I shone the light of truth on my work and realised I was deliberately covering a work colleague's lazy arse. The client had no idea he wasn't delivering, because my manager and I were doing such an awesome job of cleaning up after him, including apologising to customers who didn't receive the callbacks they were expecting and rang stressed.

Just a few days before the Amy enlightenment, I'd been talking to a close friend about how I was noticing how much energy I was spending doing stuff for other people that they could, and should, be doing for themselves. I'd been wearing an invisible superhero cape and had convinced myself I was stepping in to 'save the day', helping others avoid mistakes, pain, and awkward situations.

I could feel myself at work trying to solve problems that weren't mine to solve, trying to prove my worth when there was no proof necessary. When an email circulated asking for help, I'd routinely overextend myself to deliver above and beyond what was being asked.

When the truth of the situation was Illuminated I stood back, re-watched videos in my mind of all the ways I was *saving the day* when nobody was asking me to, and realised it was causing me significant stress and energetic depletion. No wonder I was feeling fragmented. I was handing out pieces of my time and energy like free samples at a skincare booth.

Most of all, I realised this quest to *save the day* was a complete and utter waste of time and energy. It was early September, and I made a bold spring commitment to myself to consciously step back, to take off my cape.

I thought I was over it – this need to control. I'd been calling myself a recovering control-freak Virgo for a while now. If you are a typical Virgo, or have lived with one, this needs no explanation.

What I realised was that the tendency to control was like any other addiction. You need to check in now and then, no matter how clean you think you are now or how long you've been sober. Thank goodness for my daughter Amy's wisdom.-

Stop controlling, start cultivating

There's no doubt that the Covid-19 lockdowns shed a whole new light on the concept of life control, self-determination and self-liberation. During that first lockdown period, each time I responded to the government's shifting rules and regulations by planting a simple, next-step action, I felt a little more empowered.

As the rules and regulations tightened and I stopped trying to control circumstances and simply cultivated small changes and responses, I began to feel into the small freedoms with each natural next step.

I found far more self-liberation in this than in the opposite: paralysis, fear and inaction. But there were moments throughout I'd freeze, filled with anger and frustration. And I frequently had to take my eyes and mind off the media, including social media, to feel into my decisions and plant actions for myself and my family.

There are times when taking control or gaining a sense of control is the only feasible – and often sensible – approach to a life situation. Holding on tighter can give us a sense of safety when the seas of life get rough. Even if we don't feel we can control what life's throwing at us, regaining control of ourselves and our reactions and responses to it can help us feel anchored and grounded again. Seeking control certainly has its time, place and value.

I heard many a mental health expert speak of the value of creating a routine or schedule to cope with lockdowns and stay-at-home orders, especially for those working at home and homeschooling. What I found, watching and listening to myself and those around me, was that routine was not enough.

Although there is a lot of sense in that approach, we're all wired differently, and some people thrive on both routine *and* spontaneity, structure *and* freedom. In my family's first experience of lockdown,

I noticed a desperate need for social connection and creative expression in both my girls.

Our Covid cultivation story

Two days before the first lockdown, we put our key in the door of our new holiday home on the New South Wales south coast. With rumours circulating that non-essential travel would soon be a fineable offence, we hauled our girls from our Blue Mountains rental down the coast for a lockdown adventure.

The panic set in when the girls realised the end date for lockdown was unknown and their closest friends were seven hours away. Like all families, we have a Covid-19 story, but what I'd like to share with you now is what we managed to plant and what grew and harvested for each of us.

For Lily (a senior high school student), what we **planted** was the possibility that she could leave us and our south coast home and return to school immediately by staying in a friend's granny flat for 6-8 weeks, while we sorted tenants for the south coast home. What **grew** was her deep satisfaction in experiencing her dream of independent living. What she **harvested** was the experience of that in a safe and caring environment, which resulted in her choosing – with confidence and courage – to take on her first lease (granny flat in her name), for her final year of high school in 2021.

For Amy, what we **planted** was the possibility that she could do her final year of primary school in our new beachside town and make new friends before starting high school. What **grew** from the three months down south during Covid was a deep love of her cool new town, a couple of new neighbourhood friends and a willingness to start afresh. (She flat out refused the idea of moving away when it was first put to her.) What she **harvested** was a profound sense of resilience and adventure that saw her conquer some of her biggest fears and physical challenges.

For Guy (my darling workaholic husband), what we **planted** was the possibility that the sea change could be the perfect time for his retirement. What shifted and **grew** in him was the ability for less doing and more dreaming about what a gearchange (he loves motorbikes) beach life could bring him. What he's **harvested** so far is a willingness to slow down, and accept that he's loved and appreciated far more for who he is than what he does.

For me, what was **planted** was the liberating realisation I am a LifeGardener, able to design, plant, grow and cultivate a beautiful, abundant life under any circumstances. What **grew** from that was the desire to write and share this book. It's hard to put into words what I have **harvested,** though I do try later in the book.

Although circumstances changed for all of us through these times, what remained was the practice of conscious cultivation. There's a freedom, I've discovered, in planting just one foot in front of the other; this is true for both my own decisions and choices, and those I see the people I love making and taking. Even the most difficult, challenging steps and choices seem to have both more ease and more power when your mind, heart and eyes are open, and your natural next steps are cultivated with consciousness.

Cultivation is creative

Cultivation is a creative approach to the chaos and unknowns of life. It's about seeing yourself as a LifeGardener, with the ability to consciously choose what to grow next in yourself and your life.

Cultivation allows us to say, "Yes, this is happening, but I'm going to take a few moments here and now to decide what I'm going to cultivate in response to it." Cultivation brings choice, and while we have choices, we have freedom.

Taking time to consciously cultivate our responses to what is happening in our lives – within us and around us – can mean the difference between surviving and thriving. We can respond from a place of power, not react from a place of panic.

Deciding what to *plant next* can happen in a split-second instinctive moment. Equally, taking all the time you need to sit with what's true for you can result in planting something authentic and meaningful, simply because you chose to let the idea ripen in its own time.

When you realise there are times when you can control and times when you can choose to cultivate, you begin to embrace the truth we are all co-creators, co-gardeners. When we seed and plant our deeper intentions and dreams, nature and life can play a big role in helping them to grow and bloom.

Nature's ripening

Whether you believe in universal support, angelic assistance, the Great Mystery or simply wonder at the divine timing of nature, there is no denying that to grow and cultivate anything in life, having an attitude of co-creation and co-cultivation reduces stress and brings more ease and joy.

Although I use LifeGardenening tools to cultivate change – intention seeding, weeding out what's not working, composting the past to feed the future, harvesting – there is also a surrendering to nature and life that feeds and waters this process and gives it both authenticity and power.

Just as the sun, the rain, the bees and the soil feed and nourish the garden, so too does the natural rhythm and flow of life support what you wish to grow inside yourself and in your life.

Now I have experienced living as a LifeGardener, I will never again imagine I control the outcomes of all my actions, all my plantings. I have witnessed too many examples of life, nature and the universe supporting me; I know what it feels like to plant, grow and cultivate *with* the flow of life.

Whenever I am struggling because something isn't growing my way in my time, I try to remember to step back, release my grip and feel into my old need to control so I can recognise and release it. It feels like the moment when you unkink a garden hose and, finally, things are flowing again.

When I get stuck – my hose gets kinked – I ask myself, "What am I trying to cultivate here?" The old me would push hard for an outcome, barge through delays and barriers, strive for results, never questioning why I am pushing so hard against the flow of life.

The difference between control and cultivation is all about how we respond to what's happening in ourselves and the world around us. When we feel the need to control, we tend to do one of two things: hold on tight and try to remain unchanged in our response; or react quickly to stop what's happening, though often it's out of our sphere of control.

When we pause and respond from a place of consciousness, we can shift our energetic response from contracted and fear-based to one that is expansive and open to possibility, growth and abundance.

Is there a kink in your hose?

Is there something in your life that you've been struggling with that feels like a kinked hose, as if life just isn't flowing through it? Is there a way you could release that kink and allow things to flow again?

Let it go, let it grow

If what you're trying to plant over *here* isn't taking root, or growing, let it go, let it be. Try to focus your attention on another garden bed in your life. There is always something meaningful calling for your attention.

Often, when you turn your attention away from forcing growth, you can return to that garden bed later to find either something beautiful has grown without your focus and help, or you've gained a new perspective on the situation.

This was happening with my gorgeous girls. Amy's beautiful wake-up call echoed what my instinct was telling me: I needed to step back and give my girls room to grow and blossom. I was smothering my mothering, *overwatering* my children if you like, and wondering why they weren't responding. All they really needed was for me to step out of their sunshine and fresh air, let them find their roots and let nature take its course.

This theme has revealed itself as truth in many garden beds of my life. No doubt it's proof of how controlling I have been in many areas. The most incredible growth and positive change I've seen in my life since claiming my LifeGardener powers has come from a place far from control – surrender. It's become clear to me that when my Intentions are clear and true, the potential to grow something wildly beautiful and abundant is inherent within those seeds.

I say wildly beautiful and abundant because I am constantly delighted and in awe of the way life naturally creates something far beyond my limited imagination.

My greatest power doesn't lie in the doing and the pushing – as I used to believe it did – but in ensuring what I seed and plant comes from a place of conscious, deeply rooted authenticity and the rich soil of my soul's desire.

When what we want to grow is clean and clear, life, nature, and the universe can support us in providing the conditions for growth and ripening.

Plant your way to power

I used to work as a project manager. I was renowned for delivering outcomes (sounds sexy, right!). I'd deliver on time, on budget. I'd meet those KPIs. What this took was a sharp mind, a tough approach and a willingness to push through to meet deadlines.

I've done my time pushing and have witnessed the power of observation – paying attention to what's growing inside myself and around me – before I decide on what to plant. It's not just about observation, though. When we pause, there's an opportunity to *feel into* what feels like the natural next step.

Living and working this way brings a liberation that the masculine strategise, plan, and implement model cannot. It leaves room for feminine wisdom, intuition and powerful in-the-moment decision making.

When you start to live from this place, as a LifeGardener, cultivating what grows with each simple decision and action you plant next, you can't help but feel your power grow.

Stepping into your full power, as a woman who knows that cultivation trumps trying to control the chaos of life, is one of the greatest feminine superpowers available. Consciously cultivating builds self-confidence, self-trust and intuition.

Your Cultivation journey can start with subtly shifting from relying on a tight schedule and long to-do list to checking in with yourself in the morning with simple questions like these:

- What needs watering? What's in greatest need of my attention today?

- What would feed me best today? (Based on how I feel this morning - physical energy and emotional/ mental state - what do I need?)

- What will I cultivate today?

You'll notice I asked, "What will I cultivate?" rather than "What will I do?" I ditched the to-do list a while ago because it was long and boring and never ended. Every time I crossed something off, I'd add another.

Today I use what I call a Daily Planter. Whenever I add anything to this list for the day, I ask myself why I'm doing it. It makes me stop for a moment and ask what I am trying to grow and cultivate. Sometimes I decide it isn't important enough to make the list, or I lift and replant it on another day. If you'd like to know more about my Daily Planter and try it for yourself, you can find a free downloadable copy on my website, along with a short explainer video: *www.LifeGardener.com.au/free*

Control freak confessional

If you're as cool as a cucumber, rarely stress and don't recognise yourself as being even slightly controlling, I won't be offended if you skip this part. For the rest of us – *we know who we are* – I want to take a few moments to share a couple of ways I took control-freak to a whole new level.

Pack-drill holidays

Honestly, I'm embarrassed to share. You see, the strengths of the Virgo include: planning, list-making and checking, symmetrical stacking and packing, crisis planning, culling, simplifying, organising and reorganising.

With all these superpowers packed into one starsign, you can see where packing a short segment of your life into small bags and a small car is an appealing challenge for the Virgo. And that could all go smoothly if the other people involved in the packing were unopinionated, willing to be ordered around, clear and precise about what they needed to pack, packed their crap on time and, most importantly, were enthusiastic about – and on totally on board with – Virgo leadership.

In our old family packing story, as the deadline for leaving drew near and family members (no names) started changing their minds about what they needed and didn't need, and there's fighting over legroom versus extra crap – it usually went one of two ways. Either I'd step the military-style packing sergeant gig up a notch and start screaming orders, or I throw in the towel and give up on the troops, making statements like, "Well, if you haven't packed all you need by now, don't blame me when you run out of underwear."

Whichever way it went, it wasn't pretty. Packing for holidays used to bring out my controlling worst. And with little or no help from the ex-husband, the whole debacle just felt like we were taking our same shit to a nicer location.

(In the interest of personal transformation – yours and mine – you'll be happy to hear I no longer give a crap about who's forgotten what. As long as I can see out the rear vision mirror and nobody dies on the trip... all good!)

Pre-party clean up

My old neighbour Sally was a woman who knew how to put on a party. Despite having a full-on career as a teacher, a sometimes-absent husband and three kids, she always seemed to have the time and energy to host awesome parties that ended in late-night disco ball dance-offs.

She told me one of the things that excited her most about a party was that it gave her an excuse to boss her husband and children into help cleaning up the house, perhaps even finishing bits of home handiwork. She was clever at selling the idea that the family would benefit from pitching in for the big shindig.

I can admit now I was jealous of Sally's energy, her awesome parties, magically made food and her seemingly endless enthusiasm for social gatherings. I was never Sally. I too loved getting the house party-ready, I loved cooking up and sharing good food with people and watching them delight in the colours, the smells and the connections and warmth of our house.

I'm not sure if it was the lack of pre-party alcohol that did it, but I'd always got lost somewhere between scrubbing the toilet bowl, vacuuming, finishing the decorations and laying out the starters... I'd lose the energy, vitality and joy.

I wasn't letting the excitement of the party drive my energy and lift me to party heights. I was sliding down the perfection ladder, noticing all the things I hadn't finished the way I wanted to, getting pissed off about all the help I didn't get along the way.

Those joy thieves – resentment, impatience and perfection – would steal away the moments I wished I could have stopped, taken a breath (perhaps a stiff drink), and said, "What the hell, that'll do, let's party!"

When we held Amy's 11th birthday sleepover party with nine fifth-graders, there were three things I did differently that transformed the experience for me, and I'm sure the kids:

- I started the party late Saturday afternoon. I made a pact with the family that we'd all have a lazy morning and wouldn't start cleaning and party prep until 1pm. Best decision – we were all fresh by party time.

- I said No! to WiFi. When the tweens with devices asked for our WiFi password so they could waste hours sharing social media memes, I simply said no. Stress gone!

- I had a day spa soak after. When everyone left the next day and all grew quiet, I took my tired body into a deep warm bath with candles and music.

These simple ideas were planted and grew awesome results because my party Intention was relaxation and fun, *not* perfection.

Cultivate body truth

Have these confessionals sprouted seeds of truth in you?

As you read them, did you feel a physical reaction in any part of your body? Did your neck tighten, your stomach knot? Or perhaps you just felt really uncomfortable or embarrassed for me.

I believe the body tells our emotional and soul-body truth. I also believe when we over-control, or even think about over-controlling, the body tightens, stiffens, or twists in some way.

The body understands what the mind often does not. Although our brain sits within the skull, our thinking mind has a network of nerves that extend throughout the body. We experience this through things like butterflies in the stomach, sweaty palms, a tight neck, or an uneasy feeling.

It's like an irrigation watering system that sits deep within the soil and slowly gives each part of the garden the water it needs to grow and flourish. Our bodies are also attuned to the seasons and the weather of our lives, knowing when it's time to rest and time to grow and blossom.

There's a wisdom within the body that is undeniable. The messages from our body are worth listening to. Body truth reveals what's not right for you, brings clarity about what is, and offers the freedom to choose it.

Listening well to our body's wisdom doesn't mean we have to act in response to every signal we receive. The information we receive is intelligence that reveals our deeper truths in any situation or challenge we face.

We all have at least one story of a time in our lives we've ignored our body's intelligence and convinced our mind there's a different story. (Ignoring what my body told me saw me long overstay jobs and relationships, even friendships).

In the days that lead up to my conversation with Amy – where she shone the light of truth on my controlling behaviour – I could feel my body contracting. I felt like I was riding life too high in the saddle, trying to seek answers before questions were asked, fixing things without being asked, and finishing sentences for others.

There was a tension throughout my mind and body I now recognise as the opposite of ease and grace. It manifested through my body as a stiff neck, and an impatience and discomfort in my own skin, like an itch that couldn't be scratched.

One of the beautiful things about being a conscious LifeGardener is that you practice observation of what's growing in your world and within yourself. This observation is a witnessing that allows you to make decisions about your natural next step and what you want to plant next. When you *observe* what's really growing and showing in yourself or your life, you're in a more powerful position to cultivate what comes next. There is no conscious cultivation without observation. Observation *is* consciousness.

Planting new habits, attitudes and actions from a place of eyes-and-heart-wide-open observation and truth, brings far more power and freedom than trying to *control* life's circumstances and chaos ever will.

LifeGardening Exercise

CULTIVATING BODY WISDOM

Take a few minutes to explore your body's reaction to your desire to control what's growing in the garden beds of your life.

Find a quiet, grounded space – perhaps in a garden or by a window – where you can take a few minutes to relax and tune into yourself before beginning.

Grab your list or drawing from the exercise in part two. Choose an area of your life you feel the least satisfied with, like you have little control, like it's overgrown with weeds. It might be something you've been neglecting or ignoring. Expand on what you've written or drawn by writing more about what's going on here. Try not to judge yourself, others or the situation. Write until you feel done.

Then ask yourself the following questions:

- How do I feel about this area of my life?
- How does the situation reflect what I do and don't want in my life?
- How is my body responding and reacting to this?
- What is my body wisdom telling me?

Part Three Harvest

Let's recap what we've cultivated in Part Three:

- **Stop controlling, Start cultivating.** There are times when taking control or gaining a sense of control is the only feasible – and often sensible – approach to a life situation. Holding on tighter can give us a sense of safety when the seas of life get rough. But, when you stop trying to control circumstances and simply cultivate small changes and responses, you can find small freedoms with each *natural next step*.

- **Cultivation is creative.** Cultivation is a creative approach to the chaos and unknowns of life. It's about seeing yourself as a LifeGardener, with the ability to consciously choose what to grow next in yourself and your life.

- **Let it go, let it grow.** If what you're trying to plant over *here* isn't taking root or isn't growing, let it go, let it be. Try to focus your attention on another garden bed in your life. There is always something meaningful calling for your attention.

- **Plant Your way to power.** When you start to live from this place, as a LifeGardener, cultivating what grows with each simple decision and action you plant next, you can't help but feel your power grow.

- **Cultivate body truth** - the messages from our body are worth listening to. Body truth reveals what's not right for you, brings clarity about what is, and offers the freedom to choose it.

"Learn from the flowers.
Every day is a new opportunity to experience,
to grow towards the light."

Anonymous

PART FOUR

FLOURISH

FLOURISH

n.

To be nourished in mind, body and spirit and organically bloom into being, feeling fulfilled and nurtured.

In late October 2020, a rare and precious opportunity presented itself: I had almost five full days and nights alone at home. If you're a mother, you'll get the rare and precious bit. What could I do with this all this time and space? Dive deeply into writing this book? Clean the house from top to bottom? Finish my taxes? Write my new business plan? Create my website?

I was doing that thing we do, as women, when we're gifted some spare time: fill it with stuff! What I didn't plan was a trip to the emergency department of the local hospital with what turned out to be a kidney stone. My naturopath later described the pain of a kidney stone as exquisite, and it really was as close to labour pains as I've experienced.

As the pain subsided and I contemplated all I could achieve with an almost empty house, what dawned on me was that what I needed most of all was some simple self-nourishment. The kidney stone was my body's clear sign I was overdoing work and life.

I set myself a simple, yet powerful Intention – a five-day Sensual Awakening. It's a process I love and have always gained huge benefits from. The idea is simple: every day for five days, you focus on awakening one of your five senses. The purpose is to give your tired mind a break and live your day through that sense. The senses open a divine doorway to joy and pleasure, which is beautiful. But it's also a powerful way to rekindle the mind-body connection and return you to the present moment.

I knew I could use this sensual practice to reset, relax and potentially heal my tired, exhausted mind and body. And, as much as I could dive into my to-do list, (yes, I still had one at that stage), my intuition knew the sensual Awakening would bring the energy, drive and passion I needed to thrive. I'm going to share some of the experiences from the first few days with you, and if it awakens a desire in you, I'll share more of the five-day Sensual Awakening at the end of Part 4.

DAY 1

Sense of Smell – intention: enjoy the fragrance of the day

The idea was to follow my nose through my day, experiencing as much as possible through my sense of smell. I pierced the skin on my morning lemon (for my water) and inhaled the fresh citrus essence; enjoyed the aromas of my morning skincare routine; smelt my outdoor incense from 50 metres away; sprinkled uplifting essential oil onto the steamy shower floor; went looking for flowers during work breaks; found foul smells in the street; enjoyed my food more because I was mindful to smell and taste all at once.

There were two things I noticed most of all: awakening my sense of smell naturally began to awaken my other senses; when I had work breaks throughout the day and shifted from thinking (laptop work) to being (sense focus), it was like being hit by a sensual tsunami. The day reminded me of how much I love using aromatherapy – essential oils and nature smells – to lift my energy or calm my mind and being.

DAY 2

Sense of Sound – intention: listen deeply and enjoy the silence

It had been at least a year since I'd experienced a silence retreat weekend. With my teen around for part of the day, I knew I'd only have a few hours for silence. The first few hours of the day I consciously slowed my mind, noticing every sound I could: the morning chorus, distant traffic, chickens scrapping, an unlucky snail crunching underfoot, the whirling wind, and cicada song.

The few hours of silence were challenging. When you go into silence at retreat, the idea is to not just stop talking, but to quieten the chatter of the mind. The creative inspiration for this book was flowing beautifully and I was concerned I would *squash* the flow – crimp the hose so to speak – and it would stop.

Each time I tried to quieten my mind, a new idea or line would pop into my head. When I asked myself, "Should I ignore the creative inspiration for three hours?" I knew the answer before I finished the question. *Allow, rather than ignore. Allow the flow to flow and trust it will return.*

In the afternoon following my silence, I noticed myself listening deeply during the few conversations I had. I also noticed I was listening to my body when it asked me to rest, sit, lie down, or take it easy. The day brought many gifts, including a few moments of solo dancing with headphones on while my daughter and her friend studied – I rekindled my relationship with Spotify and rediscovered my playlists. It was joyful.

DAY 3

Sense of Touch – intention: feel my way through the day.

Living on an acre in a large, soon-to-be-demolished ashram house with European arch windows, a spiral staircase, rows of fruit trees and large feature gum trees was a most unexpected and divine opportunity. On this day of touch, I finally stopped admiring just the look and smell of springtime here and headed out to explore the property.

I soaked my feet in the early morning grass, felt the newly emerging figs and kiwifruit, pulled potatoes from the veggie patch, then reached in to pull a few weeds, and quickly retracted from a sharp nettle sting, requiring frozen vegetable treatment to soothe the skin. I walked in the midday rain, umbrella free; stroked my affection-hungry puppy for much longer than I usually do; napped when my body felt tired.

What I began to notice by day three was a slowing of my mind and a growing sense of calm. Every time I returned from my practical, thinking mind back into the present moment through my sense of the day, I felt like I had nowhere else to be and nothing else to do. Right here right now was perfect.

These days of sensual awakening may sound completely foreign or indulgent to you, and about as far away from your everyday as you can get. The truth is it's foreign and rare for me, too. When life gets busy, it's easy to forget we are human *beings,* not human doings. Often, we're so far removed from our human beingness, our sensual self, that we need a deep experience – or a hospital trip – to bring us back to it.

In this part, we'll look at why it's important to take time to self-nourish if we want our health and our life to flourish. We'll look at ways of finding our unique balance between being busy and being calm and present, and why listening to what we need to survive and thrive is the starting point of self-nourishment.

Survive or thrive

It's incredible how, as women, we can get so caught up with *all there is to do,* that we forget to do the absolute basics for ourselves. Do you ever find yourself suffering from severe brain fog because you haven't eaten, or had little sleep, or both? Do you ever need dizzy spells or headaches – or a kidney stone emergency in my case – to remind you to drink more water? Have you ever put a super healthy dinner together for your toddler, then got by yourself on coffee and chocolate?

As women, we are amazing at multi-tasking, meeting deadlines, enduring pain, exhaustion and heartache. In my experience, it can come at a high price in terms of physical and/or mental health.

We are so good at just getting on with stuff, so incredibly strong and resilient, that we can ignore our body's signs and soldier on. Our body and mind talk to us every single day, dropping subtle hints we often ignore. Tight neck, stiff back, monkey mind, dry eyes, headache, restlessness, anxiety, stressed gut, sore throat, stiff joints… the list goes on. When we don't listen, our body turns up the volume.

What an incredible design, this body and mind we have. Our emotional, mental and physical being are so divinely connected and fine-tuned. It's easy to get caught just in our thoughts, to split our attention between several things and drive up the stress hormones, ignoring the signs to slow down or simplify.

My Five-Day Sensual Awakening reminded me, that when we live too much of our lives inside our head, we can close the shutters on the beautiful world that exists around and within us.

Just as a plant wilts and fades without basic food and water, so do we. It may not appear so on the outside – we're so good at faking it, right! – but the wearing effects of adrenalin overload, and mental and physical exhaustion can manifest in many ways. Excess cortisol can cause fatigue, insomnia, anxiety, burnout or a host of other similar symptoms.

So, if I asked you what you need to survive, would you instantly list food, water and sleep, or would your answer be more specific? More importantly, how do you know when you're not getting what you need? What are the signs, and do you pay attention?

Here are some of my most basic needs and the signs I'm not getting them met:

- **H20** – I learnt that lesson the hard way with the recent hospital visit. If I'm starting to feel cranky, restless or headachy, I usually need water.
- **Fresh vegetables** – I make these a daily staple, but if I go a couple of days without vegetables I just don't feel right in my body or mind.
- **Sleep** – what I need can change, but when I know I need more sleep I do whatever I can to make it happen. I nap without a hint of guilt! If I let myself get too exhausted, I become an absolute fire-breathing bitch.
- **Quiet time** – when I'm mentally overwhelmed, I need some quiet, from others and my busy mind. It doesn't take much quiet time these days – even 10 minutes alone in a day - for me to reset and relax. A little can go a long way.

If you're well aware of what you need to get by each day and stay afloat, that's great. And if you've got things in place to make sure that happens pretty consistently, or you're in the practice of listening attentively to what your mind and body needs, fantastic!

My next question to you is, do you know what you need to thrive? There's a huge difference between getting by and surviving, and feeling healthy, energised, and inspired. Understanding what makes you thrive can mean the difference between just doing okay and enjoying, even loving, life.

The way to begin to live a full bloom life is to nourish yourself, and meet your needs and desires. Only you know what these are, which is why getting cranky, angry or pissed off because other people around you just aren't giving you the space and time you need is futile. I know, because I've experienced ROPO (Ripped Off & Pissed Off) moments many times along my motherhood journey.

Here are the seven simple rituals that help me shift from survive to thrive, by feeding and nourishing my body and soul:

- **Morning yoga** – a really simple morning stretch helps me iron out the kinks and feel physically and mentally balanced, like I *do* have a left and right side to my body. I have made up my very simple (10-15 minute) routine and move in whatever ways feel best on the day.

- **Walking** – I've always loved walking. I find it incredibly peaceful, and it always takes me somewhere new in my mind. I walk out arguments and issues and walk into new ideas and fresh solutions. I've never regretted walking; it reconnects me to nature and my simpler, less heady self.

- **Silence** – I have a rich and full working life, two very chatty and energised housemates (my partner Guy and Amy), and an often-inspired creative mind. Moments, minutes, hours and even days of silence can shift me back to centre, and ground me in what's right and real again.

- **Morning cuppa in the sun** – I love the smell of a good coffee, but my drink of choice is good quality green tea. My morning cuppa, outside with the sun on my forehead, is sacred and ritualistic time. Tea tastes different when it's sipped mindfully, slowly. Sometimes I drink from a round bowl cup with no handles, so I need to use two hands to drink, and focus on this simple, joyful experience.

- **Sacred Sundays** – I recently created an intention for my Sundays to be Sacred. The sacred nature is as much about the feeling of the day as what it is that I am doing. I consciously disconnect from busyness and reconnect with those I love. I try to avoid driving. I slow down my mind and my day and often spend an hour doing a mini at-home day spa, with a bath soak, hair and face mask. It's a powerful way for me to pause before this week rolls into the next, to deepen my awareness and consciousness. It's a *stop to smell the roses* kind of day.

- **Journaling** – I've journaled for as long as I can remember. Just opening a blank page and writing freely can bring clarity, profound understanding and freedom, or it can simply help lighten the mental load.

- **Creative expression** – writing this book is good for my soul. It's helped me fulfil a lifelong dream of sharing my writing beyond my journal, with you and other women around the world. Even deeper than that is the absolute joy of the process and the journey.

It's important for me that you know my biggest and most heartfelt wish for you in reading this book is that you find your unique pathway to freedom, to living your most authentic and deeply rich version of your one precious life. Part of finding your freedom is giving yourself permission to play and explore, as you would while wandering through a divine, scented garden.

Just as every single day is different, just as the weather and seasons are changeable, so are our needs and desires.

I was once told the only thing a woman *should* routinely do every single day is pee. Everything else is optional. I don't use the list above as something I need to tick off. My awareness of what helps me thrive allows me to pick the fruit from the Self-Nourish Tree as I need it.

My wish is that your Self-Nourish Tree begins to blossom and fruit as your consciousness deepens and self-nourishment comes naturally, served guilt-free.

Goddess in the garden

Once upon a time, I craved ocean swims, time and space to myself, and quiet weekends. Deep under the surface of my super busy life was a Goddess bursting to be free, to live life in flow. She surfaced when I emerged from a saltwater swim, when I rested in the sun, when I danced with my daughters, when I lost myself in the taste of ripe mango or the scent of a soft, pink rose.

She was the Yin to my very Yang life, a part of myself I felt I had to keep secret. If I let her run wild, then what? She wouldn't work the hours I do. She didn't understand the need for money. For a long time, I lived my Goddess nature in fragments, denying she was in fact the essence of my feminine self.

Perhaps you've denied the Goddess in yourself, perhaps for similar reasons. In recent years I've embraced the Goddess in myself, the Goddess in my LifeGarden. I welcome her intuition, her softness, her reminder that I am a human being, not a human doing. She's the one who whispers to me:

"Wait, let her speak"

"Let it go, let it be"

"Sit a while and enjoy this"

"Say yes".

I'm inviting you to do the same. To pay attention to your own deep intuition, your own softer, wiser Goddess self, to awaken her within you and welcome all the beauty and richness she can bring to your life, your LifeGarden. If it feels right, you can even awaken to her through your own Five-Day Sensual Awakening. However you choose to awaken her now, I'll remind you throughout the book to listen to her wisdom. It is only through the Goddess in your own LifeGarden that you'll enjoy the deep delights that life in full bloom brings.

Dig deeper to self-nourish

Looking closely and honestly at what makes us feel cranky or ripped off can be illuminating and potentially the root of self-liberation. What angers us reveals what we're *not* feeding ourselves.

The only way to know what makes you thrive is to pay attention, to listen to what your mind and body cry out for now or have done in the past. At the beginning of this book, I shared the SoulSeed moment where, as I drove in my driveway, I received a message from my soul or higher self about my very basic desires.

What I didn't share with you at the time – mainly because I may well have scared you off early, dear reader – is that the weeks preceding this download were a difficult, anger-filled struggle.

I was blaming other people and impacts for my anger and stress; my workload, my bosses, my partner, old boyfriends, old bosses, the weather. As I worked through and composted the layers of anger and fear, I finally took responsibility and asked my soul-self the deeper Blooming Question, "What is it you long for?"

Revelations like these can take time, and lots of ROPO moments, so be gentle with yourself along the way. When we know what we need, the next step to full bloom living it is to begin to plant the seeds for that to grow. Wishing for it – without planting it in action – won't make it grow.

Want more silence and quiet in your life? Plant some of that, like meditation, simple but not always easy. I'm going to share with you my very recent experience of finding a way to plant more grace and ease in my life.

Planting grace wasn't easy

Grace & Ease was the first of the seven SoulSeeds that sprouted that September morning. Grace & Ease showed herself as my soul's most sought-after desire. What I want in my daily life, and have always wanted my whole adult life, is a sense of Grace & Ease. She revealed herself through her opposite: stress, overwhelm and anxiety.

I asked myself where in my life I most commonly struggle with stress and overwhelm. What are those moments and situations I am finding most stressful, and where do I have the greatest potential to bring more Grace & Ease?

There were three clear leaders in the stress and overwhelm stakes:

- When I find work confusing, especially understanding what's needed, I can feel overwhelmed and stressed, especially when there's a deadline looming.

- When I feel overwhelmed by the logistics of motherhood and life management and forget to ask for help.

- When I'm having a conversation with someone who is particularly stressed or emotionally overwhelmed and I am tired or unsure of how to help and forget that just listening is often enough.

Once I was aware of the stress and overwhelm *weeds* that were growing in my LifeGarden, I needed to decide what to plant anew. I chose just three simple new Intention Seeds I could plant in action:

- **Start each day with an intention of Grace & Ease.** This requires consciously pushing aside negative and busy thoughts when I wake, saying good morning to myself and checking in with my body and mind before my feet hit the floor. It's choosing not to turn on my phone until I've woken, washed my face, and fully connected with myself, my family and the world outside.

- **Be as present as I can.** As I move through my day, I do what I can to stay exactly where I am: fully with the sunrise, fully in the conversation, fully in the document I am editing, fully with myself as each experience unfolds. This takes consciousness and practice, but it's a practice that reaps a beautiful reward. In these moments I am not fighting the reality of the present moment. This surrendering to what is unfolding is Grace & Ease for me.

- **Fully accepting what is.** One of the benefits of committing to present moment living is that you become fully aware of the many moments you would prefer were *not* happening. When you start paying attention to the way your neck tightens when you start a Zoom meeting you know will be long and boring, or the frustration that arises when you're interrupted by your child mid-thought, you can begin to see these annoyances and interruptions for what they are: absolute gifts. Fully feeling our responses opens a doorway to truth, about how we do and don't want to spend our time. That information is intelligence we can use to replant our LifeGarden. Even more profound is the shift that can happen when we soften through those annoyances and simply accept the moment as it is.

Planting practical support

All the good intentions in the world won't stand a chance against a super busy schedule. No matter how much I intended to move through my day with Grace & Ease, I knew there were some basic changes I had to make to give this SoulSeed a chance to germinate and grow in my everyday.

I asked myself what else I could do to support the growth of Grace & Ease growing. I now think of these as the four walls that border my Grace & Ease garden bed, to keep the weeds of stress and overwhelm at bay:

- **Create space between things** – sounds basic, but I do what I can to create enough room for things to flourish in my day.
- **Avoid overcrowding** – I leave room between meetings and, if people and demands are fighting for my time, I say no, and suggest replanting things replanted another time or day.
- **Discern my time and energy** – when I have a choice, I think carefully about how I spend my time and energy, rather than leaving it to others to take whatever they want and leave the scraps for me.
- **Book myself in** – I carve out time in my diary – electronic and hard copy versions – so I have the breathing, thinking, and reflection time I need within my day and week. I book myself monthly massages, weekly nature escapes and daily yoga and meditation time. I even block out decent lunch breaks throughout my work week.

Grace loves space, and so do I.

Once upon a time, I thought my need for space was selfish and indulgent. Now I know it's not only my soul's birthright, but everyone in my life and everything I do benefits from me taking the time and space I need to live my life at my natural pace, with Grace & Ease.

Self-centred living

Self-centering is not selfish. It's a healthy, natural, organic process where we can feel into what's going on in our mind-body-spirit and come back into balance. This returning to our centre is a powerful opportunity to reground ourselves – to stop the busyness and headiness and simply drop into our physical body and breath – and replant how we are living.

This was my experience with the recent SoulSeed insight. The anger and frustration, then the feeling into and asking my soul for truth, left room for sifting through the details of how I was spending my time and energy. But it's not just a balancing of what you are doing, but of who you are being. And the sifting and replanting left me feeling more deeply rooted in the earth of who I am.

This has nothing to do with work-life balance and everything to do with self-balance, listening deeply to your own needs and placing yourself at the centre of your life. This is a conscious practice and requires a devotion to self-truth.

Imagine yourself as a divine mosaic Goddess sculpture hiding in the corner of your LifeGarden, covered in weeds, her light and beauty unseen. You have the power to release that Goddess, free her from weeds and neglect, let the rain wash her clean, and have her moved to the middle of your luscious LifeGarden, where she can radiate beauty.

Being centred makes you stronger and more balanced, less likely to be knocked over by disturbances and disruptions. It's also a beautiful, authentic place to be. When we practice self-centring, the ROPO (Ripped off, Pissed Off) state is far less likely, as our practice and devotion pull us back to our centre with a natural Grace and Ease.

Yin yang balance

Imagine yourself in an exquisite Japanese garden in the springtime. Bright red cherry trees in full bloom against the blue sky, large feature rocks on white pebbles next to soft, slow-moving water, giant orange fish swimming under quaint wooden bridges. What works beautifully in such gardens, and sings to our soul, is the tranquillity that comes when hard (tree, rock, stone, bridge) meets soft (blossoms, fish, water, shrubs). When designed with this balance in mind, the result is exquisite, perfect and soothing.

The fact that we can create and appreciate this exquisite balance and ease naturally leads to the possibility that we can experience it in our mind and lives. Imagine how our daily lives would change if we could choose to return to that sanctuary at any time. I believe we can.

When the term work-life balance was hitting the mainstream, there were all sorts of debates going on about the perfect balance for working women. I was new to the working mum thing and returned to full-time work when Lily was only four weeks old. This was not my plan. But, as life had it, I found myself earning the money and pumping breastmilk in the ninth-floor work bathroom.

What I know now is that no article, study, expert or schedule can tell me what it is I need to feel a sense of balance in my life. What works for one woman won't necessarily work for another. What energises one woman can deplete another. Just the nature of the word balance suggests a state of Nirvana, a perfect formula, can be reached – and then what?

The most liberating insight I received about this life balance thing is so profoundly simple it'll blow your mind.

Listen to yourself (your heart, your mind) and ask what it is you need right now: more yin or more yang?

If you think back to that exquisite Japanese garden, yang is represented by the harder elements, yin by the softer ones. In human terms, we're in yang when we're productive, active, questioning, working, and doing. We're in yin when we're quiet, reflective, still, sensually awake, open-hearted, generous, and present. Yang watches the clock: yin doesn't.

Some people refer to this balance as masculine (yang) and feminine (yin) energies. Typically, we spend far more time in the masculine yang than the feminine yin. For women who are *balancing* being a mother, partner, professional, it's easy to tip the balance way into the yang. Personally, my biggest struggles and resentments as a mother have been knowing deep down that I wanted to spend more time with baby on breast and less time bringing in the bacon – more yin, less yang.

For me, yang imbalance shows up when I'm just doing too much, as tiredness, restlessness, crankiness, short-temper, short attention span, and a desire to run away and hide like a bear in a cave. Sometimes all it takes is a long hot bath, a 10-minute meditation or a short walk. Other times when I know I'm coming up to a busy week, I'll mix up my gentler yin with my bigtime busy yang days.

When I know I'm in need of some yin time, I do one or more of the following:

- Go to bed early (alone if I need to) and/ or sleep in
- Go for a walk in nature
- Have an afternoon nap
- Listen to some relaxing music or meditation tracks
- Sit in a café or by a lake reading a (non-work) book
- Hang out with the dog
- Flaneur for a day*

Flaneur is my favourite French word (I don't know many). It translates as: a person who strolls a promenade with no fixed program. When you spend a day or an afternoon *a la flaneur,* you wander through the streets, shops, markets or gardens, with no agenda, no deadline and no particular place to go or be. You people-watch, you observe, you enjoy the sights around you. It's like being on holiday but you can do it close to home. Shifting your mindset from "I'm ducking out to get milk and bread before I…" to "I'm heading out for a while" (or the day) is so incredibly freeing and fun. And you don't need to spend money to love it!

Sometimes I try on loads of outfits just for the joy of it. Sometimes I deepen the experience by deliberately awakening the senses one at a time – smell in the essential oil shop, sight in the home store or art gallery, touch in the clothing stores, sounds along the footpath, and wind up with a pocketful of local handmade chocolates to taste. It's a truly divine way to balance out those busy yang days and weeks with a big dose of yin.

Life is dynamic, organic, and so are we. It's okay to need something one day or week, and not desire it the next. It's okay to play with and be curious about what nourishes you. And it's curiosity that will lead you to discover what truly lights you up, warms your heart, and nourishes your beautiful soul.

Where's your sunshine?

I'd love to know what it is that brings you joy in your life, brings a lightness to your day, softens your heart and reminds you life is wonderful. No matter how small the joy, if it brings you sunshine, and warms you well, my wish is that your life blooms with more of what you love.

Those divine moments in our lives are not Instagrammable. The moment is too deep and beautiful to capture from the other side of the lens. Though, I do believe your camera roll can say a lot about what lights you up, and what you're drawn to.

What are those simple things that take your breath away? My guess is you're drawn to nature and life's most natural moments. Whatever those divine and meaningful things are, my simple message is this: do, have, and experience more of that!

As a LifeGardener, when you begin to pay attention to the parts of your life that bring greatest joy, satisfaction, laughter and richness, life begins to bring your more of the same. In the garden that is your life, your attention is like the sun. What you choose to shine it towards will grow and bloom.

It's easy to forget, and find yourself back on the treadmill of life. For the days and weeks roll by at great speed, with little or no time to spend in the sunshine. As you now know, the key to LifeGardening is consciousness, staying awake. And realising when you're on that treadmill again shows that you are awake and aware of when you want to slow down, step off and enjoy the sunshine.

One simple way to do this is to cultivate morning and evening rituals that support you in growing the kinds of days you want to experience.

Nourishing AM

No two days are the same, especially when it comes to motherhood. I'm not a coffee girl, but I can appreciate the need almost every woman I know has for a good strong coffee to function and get through the day. Apart from coffee, what do you need to start the day? 10 minutes without talking to another human, bathroom time alone, a good stretch or a run?

If you could completely create and cultivate your morning, what would it look and feel like? Take a few minutes to daydream about this. What could you do between when you wake and when the world outside needs you that would truly nourish you?

My daydream was waking early, lemon water and morning yoga, followed by a brisk walk on the beach, light breakfast with the family and a writing session before the world outside needed me. This daydream is now my (almost) everyday reality.

At the time when this daydreaming began – almost 20 years ago – I was waking exhausted from night-time breastfeeding, dressing with my eyes closed and commuting by crowded bus through peak hour traffic to scoff Turkish toast before my first meeting.

No matter what your AM reality is now, you can begin to grow and cultivate a morning that nourishes and enriches you. If it's not nourishing you, pay attention to what you don't want to be experiencing. Again, remember, that the key to good gardening is observation.

To get what you want, to cultivate mornings that nourish you, all you need to do is plant simple seeds towards that dream. That's how we turn dreams, even small daydreams, into reality.

Nourishing PM

Creating a nourishing PM can be challenging, especially if you or others in your house are in the habit of watching Netflix or getting in some screen time last thing before bed. If you're having trouble sleeping or waking exhausted and sluggish, taking a close look at your night-time wind down might be helpful. Using lamps or candles instead of bright lights, reading or listening instead of using screens, and soft music instead of loud conversation can help everyone wind down for better sleep.

Dimming the noise and lights of the day is both a literal and metaphorical exercise. The aim is to slow down and turn down the layers of noise. For me, noise and stimulation include everything from electronic devices to harsh lights, not to mention the mental chatter of my busy mind.

It's powerful to consciously slow down internal and external conversations. It can be tempting when your mind relaxes towards the end of the day to remember that intense or crucial thing you wanted to ruminate over or discuss with someone else. Tense conversations when we're tired are often overstimulating and can disturb sleep patterns, especially if they leave more answers than questions. Consider jotting these down and postponing them until the light of day.

When you're in the practice of deliberately slowing down the mind, and calming the atmosphere in the house, the benefits can be incredible. The conversations can shift and deepen, and the quiet of the night can become a welcome contrast to the busyness of the day.

This is merely an invitation for you to try something different, especially if your current evening is leaving you with a buzzing mind, frantic family and poor sleep. As always, it's all about Intention: what you want to cultivate for yourself and those around you.

As I mentioned earlier, expecting those around us to know and provide what we need is futile and can lead to deep resentment. Once you know what you want your mornings and evening to look and feel like, telling those around you about your intentions and desires can be helpful. Once they see the benefits, they may even help plant the seeds to cultivate it.

Asking your partner and/or kids for time, space, quiet or whatever else you need, even in small doses, is great *ask and you shall receive* practice.

Cultivating quiet time

Quietening the house at night, by turning down the lights, turning off screens and softening the mood is a powerful practice, even if you only do it a couple of nights a week to feel into the contrast.

It can give you an insight into the preparations that happen when you're going into a silence retreat. I've been on five or six such retreats now, all during my motherhood years; only short weekend ones.

There's no conversation, no devices, no writing (hard not to pick up a pen as a writer), and no eye contact. The eye contact thing is tricky because you want to say thank you with your eyes when some fellow silence retreater holds the door open for you.

Although every retreat experience is different, in terms of what arises in my mind and how I flow (or not) through the experience, some things remain the same. The mind is busy and chatty at the beginning, sometimes absurdly funny. But over time, the mind does slow down.

A silence retreat isn't about silencing the mind, but using the silence around you – the lack of noise and distraction – to quieten and slow the mind to its more peaceful and natural state.

For me, the focus becomes the natural sights and sounds and the key, so they say, is to observe and enjoy these without letting them send your mind on a wild over-thinking ride.

The reason I'm sharing this with you is that there are many amazing benefits to slowing and quietening the mind. If the evening at home practice feels good for you, perhaps you can try some solo silence stints as a regular practice.

Removing the layers of family and work responsibilities, pinging devices, deadlines, conversation and mental chatter – even just for an hour or two a week – can have profound positive effects on your mental health and help grow more clarity and peace.

Without a doubt, my favourite moments in this practice are those of stillness and peace, when I feel into the fact that I have nowhere to go, nothing to do, other than to be here, be still and quiet.

Want to try a mini silence retreat at home?

Step 1 – Pick a day and time when you know you'll be alone, either at home or outside in a quiet place in nature.

Step 2 – Pick your duration. Try starting with between 15 minutes and an hour if this is your first time. If you want to try longer, book in a few hours.

Step 3 – Set an alarm on your phone for your set duration then turn it to flight mode or 'do not disturb'.

Step 4 – Remove or distance yourself from all other distractions. Write down any thoughts buzzing around your mind that may distract you.

Step 5 – Move into the most calm and comfortable environment you can find (in your home or in nature) and begin by closing your eyes and taking 20 slow, deep breaths. Allow yourself to move around during your practice with ease and spontaneity. As thoughts arise, just allow them to pass by. Notice sights and sounds without engaging or analysing. Simply enjoy and allow the experience to gently unfold.

Step 6 – When your time is up, allow yourself to gently return to your day. Notice how it feels when the sights, sounds and thoughts begin to flow at normal pace. Journal your insights and plan your next mini-retreat.

Cultivating deep rest

My sister's husband once told me she only has two states: flat out busy and flat out asleep on the couch. Going until we drop seems as socially acceptable as it is common. The question, "How are you?" is often answered with, "Super busy!" or "Flat out!" The simple fact that we diarise social gatherings weeks, sometimes months in advance, says a lot about the crazy pace of our lives.

Who has time for rest and why would you bother, given all there is to do? The case for rest is simple: time spent resting gives you energy and the opportunity to heal. Just 10 minutes of deep rest can bring huge benefits.

Apart from the physiological effects such as lowering blood pressure, resting and slowing the chatty mind can let you sink deeply into your divine, natural peaceful state.

It requires a releasing of all the things you think you need to do in the future to fully surrender to the moment, minutes, or hours, you've gifted yourself as rest time.

Sitting on the couch bingeing intense drama isn't rest. It's fun, it can transport you to a fantastic world, but it's not rest. Coffee with a girlfriend can be fabulous, energising you and lifting your mood, but it's not rest. Swiping on social media lying flat on your back is not rest, even if the content is positive or lifts your mood.

Rest sounds simple, but it can be challenging to practice when you're used to productivity and multi-tasking and have trained your brain to only rest when your head hits the pillow. There's also the fear that *if I stop, I'll drop* and won't be able to get up again to get anything done.

Like you, I can push through tiredness, exhaustion even, to get things done. I can meet work deadlines, and do a 15-hour day, without a quiet moment, without a proper meal at a table. We all have that ability. My question is, "If that is how you're living most days, is that serving you, nourishing you?"

I guarantee you that a woman who is flat out busy, no matter how amazing her life may look on the outside, isn't enjoying it. It's like having a perfectly manicured garden: you never have to enjoy it, inhale its perfume, rest in its shade, taste its fruit, and pick its flowers.

Having the ability to listen to when your mind and body needs rest and giving yourself that rest is an absolute Goddess in the Garden superpower. Like all things, it takes practice. I'd like to share with you some of the simple ways I take rest: see whether any of these resonate for you:

- **Awake in bed** – especially on weekends, just a few minutes lying in bed after I wake up can be deeply restful and satisfying (not scrolling social, not creating my mental to-do list).

- **Guided meditation** – I sit quietly in the sun or somewhere comfortable and quiet and use the Calm App on my smartphone for simple, 10-minute meditations. My big white headphones tell the family I'm on 'do not disturb'. Although I usually sit, if I'm tired, I'll lay in bed or on my yoga mat to meditate.

- **Slow yoga** – slow, gentle stretches on my yoga mat, just improvising, feel fantastic. Sometimes I'll end up flat on the mat with my lavender eye bag on for a few minutes.

- **Savasana** – is a pose used at the end of many yoga classes. You simply lie flat on your back (on a yoga mat or a blanket on the floor), with your palms facing upwards, arms by your side. The aim is full body rest. I set an intention to rest deeply, including my mind. I use an alarm for 10 minutes and let any thoughts pass like clouds. If my mind starts to race, I start to count my breaths until it slows again.

- **One slow, work-free cuppa** – at least once a day I deliberately step away from the laptops and phones for a cup of my favourite green tea outside. If it's pouring rain I'll sit on the couch and enjoy the sounds. This simple ritual can reset and recharge me within minutes.

I'll say again, rest takes practice, and Intentions are powerful. If I write in the Daily Planter that day I want to take three seven-minute savasana breaks during the day to increase my energy, you can be guaranteed that in at least one of those practices my mind is racing, or I'm interrupted. But the more I practice and the simpler and truer my Intention, the greater the chance I'll reap the benefits.

If you don't already have a Goddess in the Garden rest practice, I invite you to choose one from the list above or cultivate your own. You can never have too many options. You can add your rest options to your Self- Nourish Tree.

You can download your Self Nourish Tree template and instructions from the website:

www.LifeGardener.com.au/free

Part Four Harvest

Let's recap the Part Four Flourish:

- **Survive or thrive.** The way to begin to live a full bloom life is to nourish yourself, meet your needs and desires.

- **Dig deeper to self-nourish.** Looking closely and honestly at what gives us ROPO, can be illuminating, and potentially the root of self-liberation. What angers us reveals what we're *not* feeding ourselves.

- **Self-centred living.** Self-centering is not selfish. It's a healthy, natural, organic process where we can feel into what's going on in our mind-body-spirit and come back into balance.

- **Yin yang balance.** Listen to yourself (your heart, your mind) and ask what it is you need right now: more yin or more yang?

- **Nourishing AM and PM.** If you could completely create and cultivate your morning and evening, what would they look and feel like? What could you do between when you wake and when the world outside needs you that would truly nourish you? How could you create a soft, relaxing pre-bed experience?

- **Cultivating quiet time.** Removing the layers of family and work responsibilities, pinging devices, deadlines, conversation and mental chatter – even just for an hour or two a week – can have profound positive effects on your mental health and help cultivate clarity and peace.

- **Cultivating deep rest.** Practicing deep rest requires a releasing of all the things you think you need to do in the future to fully surrender to the moment, minutes, or hours you've gifted yourself as rest time.

> "Plant so that your own heart will grow."
>
> Hafiz

PART FIVE

GROW

COMPOST YOUR PAST

n.

Any conscious practice that turns
the memories and emotions of the past into
rich and fertile soil for your future dreams and desires to grow.

If I said I have a "dream" relationship, what would your first reaction be? Would you think I'm delusional, lucky, or both? I call it that because I dreamed it up before it appeared in my reality. I saw it happen before it happened. At least I saw, very clearly, who I wanted to be, how I wanted to show up, how I wanted to *feel* in the scary depths of a true, intimate relationship.

And I was scared. I was terrified of repeating my past, staying longer than I should in relationships that made neither of us happy, enduring what I should be enjoying, *and sticking it out* like a relationship athlete. I was scared I didn't know how to love and be loved. I was afraid that what I wished for – an equal, loving, intimate, joyful partnership – was reserved for Hollywood movies and the lucky ones.

It was in my psychologist's chair that I planted a powerful Intention Seed that would instantly shift me from fear to curiosity: "I love to travel," I told her. "I love waking up in a foreign city and walking the streets, exploring the sights, the people, the smells and sounds. I've decided I'm going to see my next relationship just like that – like a trip to an unknown destination."

Just like that...

I'd been single for almost two years since the last unmentionable relationship. Before that, 15 years with the father of my two beautiful girls. Single life with my daughters was good and easy. But I felt a growing desire for intimacy I realised I had never been willing or able to show up for.

This is not a part devoted to cultivating more intimate relationships. Though if that's your heart's desire, please savour the fruits within it. It's a part I hope will Illuminate the truth of your inherent power, the seed of your liberation: you can seed, plant and grow whatever your heart desires most, whether it's more intimate relationships, effortless money flow, creative freedom, a peaceful home life, or a flourishing career.

I'm sharing my relationship seed-plant-grow story because, without a doubt, it was the garden bed most filled with big, tough weeds of shame, regret and fear. I'm sharing my insecurities, self-doubt and vulnerabilities with you as an act of faith in our connection and the transformational power of sisterhood storytelling.

Given my endurance athlete approach to relationships, I welcomed the desire emerging from within me for an unknown intimacy. I had written in my journal (months before my psychologist appointment) of this longing, and called myself out:

How long am I going to have my toes in the river of my life? When am I going to plunge into its depths, savour its nourishing and bountiful beauty? I no longer wish… to stand at the edge of the river of my life with only one toe submerged. I no longer wish… to live with doubt and fear about myself, my choices and my life. I no longer wish… to feel dissatisfied and uninspired by myself and my life.

At the age of 46, I realised I had never left or ended a relationship. My pattern was to endure until the other person left, or to have an affair, rather than painfully cut the cord. So, at the end of my 15-year relationship, aged 46, when I found myself staring into the dark abyss of the unknown, I found and spoke my painful truth.

At one point during marriage counselling, my husband asked me to commit to fixing our relationship, vowing he was committed to doing the same. But I knew my commitment was to truth. The *truth* was I needed to be free of our relationship, of any relationship, for a while. Not since I was 16 years old had I been single for more than four weeks. Mine had been a life of mostly self-inflicted misery, endured with the help of good quality alcohol, good friends and socially acceptable workaholism.

I'd mistaken sex for intimacy, and obligation for partnership. When I finally reached a point in my marriage where the fear of staying was greater than the fear of leaving, I jumped. It's true what they say: with transformation comes both liberation and loss. The sense of security, of the known, was ripped out at the roots.

In the single years that followed I had the divine space and time to plant new Intention Seeds, to consciously cultivate my self-love garden, to compost my past to feed my future. I let myself daydream and explore my vision of intimate loving relationships. I watched couples in the street connecting, caressing, kissing, embracing, and could feel the possibilities budding within me.

I was willing, despite the fear, to invite intimacy into my life – emotional, spiritual and physical. I knew some things were completely foreign to me, like staring into my lover's eyes and standing toe to toe. By permitting myself to daydream, to not just see but *feel* all the emotions that washed through me, I was literally becoming my future self.

I used my nature connection – Goddess in the Garden – as a doorway into a world of sensual and erotic possibility. Surely, if I can lose myself in the fragrance of daphne or jasmine, in the caress of the full moonlight, this intimacy and sensuality is possible with another.

I'm imagining some readers, at this point, furrowing their brow, wondering how a woman could reach her late forties and realise she's never lost herself in the eyes of her lover and melted all time and matter. Well, dear reader, I'm here to say it's possible to be so focused on cultivating some parts of your life and busying yourself, that you can ignore those garden beds filled with weeds. And the ones with the most weeds are often those with the greatest potential to bring joy and full bloom satisfaction.

I knew I would meet a man. That was inevitable. What mattered most to me was keeping the vows I had made to myself, the Intention Seeds I had planted during my year of self-love schooling. From my journal:

As I remember how to love myself I will:

- *Make choices that feel right in my head and my heart and nourish me and my relationships*
- *Forgive myself and allow authentic expression and self-love*
- *Step into the present with courage and conviction and a sense of adventure.*
- *Stand eye to eye, heart to heart, toe to toe in a space of love.*

At the same point in my journal, I found a line from Amy. She placed some unopened camellia flowers in my hand and said, I kid you not, "Mum, I'm giving these to you to remind you of who you are."

When I did meet Guy, and moved from love theory into love practice, love bloomed within and around me as effortlessly as the camellias. That's not to say I wasn't scared. After seven dates in our first week, I kept my scheduled appointment with my psychologist. She was thrilled by my pronouncement then, just minutes after we celebrated my blooming, I panicked... "What do I do now?" Then we laughed so hard that I almost fell off my chair.

It was like the end of a five-year-old's first week at school when they feel so proud that they went to school Monday to Friday, only to be told they'll be doing it again next week, and the week after, and the week after...

Seed the change

You can see where I'm heading with this, can't you?

Change – authentic, full-bloom change – only comes from within. Only when we truly envision ourselves living our dreams, and feel ourselves deep within those dreams, can they fully bloom. The most powerful seeds you will ever plant will be within the divine fertile soil of your innermost self.

Gandhi was right: "Be the change you want to see in the world." You are the gardener. Your dreams and desires fertilise the soil from which they grow. And when your actions come from that authentic place of heartfelt intention, you can grow things beyond your imaginings.

What was it I wanted to seed in myself to cultivate an authentic, loving and intimate relationship?

- **Courage** and willingness to show up
- **Self-forgiveness** when I messed up or ran away with fear
- **Presence** and willingness to stay in the moment when I felt woozy and washed over by the waves of intimacy
- **A sense of adventure** like travelling to a foreign place that is a new and exciting relationship
- **A love of love** replacing my Hollywood scepticism with real-world curiosity
- **Lightness** and a light, playful attitude to love

When I daydreamed and visioned, I saw myself showing up in this way. I permitted myself to imagine what standing face-to-face with my love would feel like, and to stay with those feelings, to practice living with courage and presence. I still draw on those feelings today, years into my relationship.

It was recently brought to my attention that I was leaving the room when the conversation became uncomfortable. Guy called me out on it, and I revisited those visions of who I wanted to be in my relationship. I realised I needed to add another layer, another scene to the *me in loving relationship* movie.

I planted a new Intention Seed and shared it with him. "I know I've been leaving when things get tough, and I just don't know what to say next. My intention is to stay, and if I need a few moments to breathe and think before I speak, I'll tell you that's what I'm doing. Sometimes I'll forget and storm off, but I'll do what I can to stay conscious."

Sometimes sharing an Intention Seed with another can be powerful, particularly if you're trying to change the way you react to a familiar situation. In relationships, it's easier to fall into *ever/ always/ never* language: "You always act that way… You never listen to me… Why don't you ever…?" As women, we can be incredibly sharp at this, at pulling the past out of our mental filing cabinet. It's almost a superpower! But, let's face it, it's rarely helpful.

Sometimes when we try to vision or imagine ourselves in full bloom in an area of our lives, we can feel like an undeserving fraud. It's hard to imagine yourself receiving great things and loving your life if you're just not feeling it. If you find yourself stuck with this visioning and feeling process, this may be due to one of the following:

- **Visioning practice** – if you're just not used to daydreaming and visioning, that's okay. Like all new things, visioning takes practice. I'll give you the opportunity to play more with this.

- **Not into your vision** – perhaps you're just not motivated to make any changes in that part of your life right now. If your heart's not in it, you just won't *feel it*. That's useful information for you. Maybe what you've been growing is rooted in someone else's beliefs or obligations.

- **Something is holding you back** – sometimes the reason we're unable to grow something new is that we're relying on past, outdated beliefs and fears to feed and fertilise our present. If that feels true for you, it might be time to look at the benefits of composting.

Compost your past to feed your future

I want you to consider the possibility that our past can and does feed our future. Just sit with it for a minute or two. Ask yourself whether you believe this to be true. It's universally accepted that our past influences our future, plays a role, and has an impact. But the words *feed your future* say something far richer: that if we compost the past, rather than let it sit and rot, cause a stench or leave us paralysed with fear, it can enrich the soil of our dreams and desires, remind us of what we do and don't want in our lives and help us grow a better future.

Creating good compost is all about having just enough air, turning and mixing, and just enough carbon and nitrogen to break down the old and turn it into quality food and nutrients.

Our emotional past is no different. Too much attention and too much digging can lead to living in and growing from the past. We want just enough emotional turning to draw out what's useful and helpful. Much of this happens naturally, unconsciously, as we grow and evolve. But sometimes we need some help with the process. This is particularly true if we're leaving a trail of compost all over our LifeGarden and relationships.

My psychologist was a perfect example of this – someone I could trust to help me compost my past relationship experiences, draw out the nutrients to feed my future, and plant new Intention Seeds, such as seeing a new relationship like travelling to a new country.

Stepping through a composting process with a professional can be fruitful and nourishing (and safer) if it feels right for you. Although I'm sharing the intimacies of my relationships with you here, these same principles apply to any area of your life – money, career, motherhood, creativity, education, friendships – any garden bed in which you wish to seed-plant-grow something new.

There are other ways you can compost your past to feed your future. My experience of what I now term composting has come in several forms:

- **Journaling** – when it comes to the journal, it's as much about the journey as the destination. Simply putting pen to paper can reveal incredible insights and wounds and you'll often end up in a place of fresh perspective and clarity.

- **Burning it off** – sometimes writing then burning what you've written to *let it go* can be symbolically and emotionally powerful. Of course, be careful where and how you burn, safety first always. I've had some of my most cleansing and healing evenings throwing old journal notes into my fire in the mountains.

- **Deep conversation** – even if you're not seeing a professional, a trusted friend can be a wonderful listener and mirror for you. My advice would be to let them know what your intention is, such as, "I'm hoping to explore my history around [insert subject] and I'd love it if you'd just sit with me and listen." You can always invite their feedback and return the favour by letting them do the same to clean out and compost some part of their own LifeGarden.

- **Timeline exploration** – one day I took a couple of hours to timeline all the (attempted) intimate relationships I could recall in my lifetime. I drew them on a line from five years old to the present, plotted the good, the bad, and the ugly, and then felt into them one at a time, jotting down the things I learnt about myself and love along the way.

This last exercise may sound like a big commitment timewise. What it gave me was a profound insight into my patterning in relationships, plus the obvious surface-level *aha realisation* that I'd rarely been single my entire life.

Want to plant a timeline?

You can timeline any pattern or event in your life: work, creative projects, travels, house moves, friendships. You'll be surprised what you can uncover. If you want to try this, you can either start from your earliest or most recent recollection. You can map out things as they come to mind first and then plot them on a timeline. Here are some simple steps:

Step 1 – Decide what area of your life you want to timeline

Step 2 – Grab a piece of paper and pen and write your subject in the middle of the page, then circle it.

Step 3 – Using a mindmap style, draw lines off the circle to create other circles or topics that are related. These might be events, conversations, turning points, losses or gains.

Step 4 – Write down any insights that come from this process. Keep going until you feel done.

Step 5 – Draw a timeline from as far back as these memories and events go to today and plot what you've dug up in your mindmap.

Step 6 – Take a broad look at all you have experienced in this part of your life. What have you learnt about yourself and your experiences? Share the exercise with someone you trust if you feel it's appropriate and helpful.

Composting your past can ultimately bring self-liberation, not only because you're accepting the past as the past, but because you're finding its inherent value for the future, with the intention to do better when you know better.

When we compost the past, inevitably we'll also uproot feelings of guilt, shame or regret, and a psychologist or trusted therapist can assist greatly in this process. But when we dig in and compost with a clear intention to reveal the learnings, something shifts in the process. My own experience holds truest to this – Intention is everything.

Plant powerful intention seeds

I know we planted the concept of Intention Seeds earlier in this book, but I want to dive deeper and enrich your understanding. Let's look at what makes an Intention Seed powerful and well worth planting.

Remember, an Intention Seed is something you intend to plant in yourself or your life to grow something different or better. Its potency comes from the fact that it is infused with inherent meaning personal to you. There are generally three types of Intention Seeds: one-off Actions, new Habits, and Attitude shifts.

In my experience, the more authentic and heartfelt your Intention, the more likely it will germinate and grow into something beautiful or wondrous, with little effort or *work* on your part.

Lots of things will grow and show in our lives just because we make an effort, whether or not we care about them. We can win a race because we've trained, even if our hearts are unmoved. We can pass a test because we've studied hard. We can save up for a new car, solve complex problems, do just about anything.

PART FIVE: GROW

All that is required is two things:

- ♣ A goal or focus
- ♣ Commitment

Knowing we can do almost anything we put our mind and time to, the question becomes, "What do I want to put my heart into? What do I really want and desire?" When we become clear about what's in our heart and what we desire in any area of our life, that Intention becomes nourished with high intensity, love-infused, nutrient-rich superfood.

Let's take an example from your own life for a moment, sweet bloomer. Let's revisit that area of your life you identified earlier, the one where you were most wanting and willing to change your attitude, your behaviour or your LifeGarden state.

Grab your journal and pen and write down a few words that describe it. To seed the change you want to be, write down what you saw yourself doing and being in your Vision. If you need to, close your eyes again for a few minutes and reVision or daydream.

What are you doing? How are you being? How does it feel in your body? As your Vision becomes clear, so will the Intention Seeds you may wish to plant to grow the Vision into reality. I invite you to relax throughout this process and allow your intuition to lead.

Here are some sample Vision statements to feed and fertilise your process:

- ♣ **Money freedom Vision:** "Money is flowing easily through my life and I am finding new financial freedoms every day."
- ♣ **Intention Seeds (actions/ habits):** Put my bills on autopay, set up auto savings, and start Money Hour Mondays.

- **Intention Seeds (attitudes):** Create weekly money mantras, track and welcome all money and gifts.

- **Relaxed Motherhood Vision:** "I love my time with my kids, and make sure I nourish myself well so I can be fully present with them."

- **Intention Seeds (actions/ habits):** Nap when I need to, give them 'special time', and meditate with headphones.

- **Intention Seeds (attitudes):** Sink into special moments, and let the housework go when I want to.

- **Deeper friendship Vision:** "I am cultivating deeper friendships by listening well, with genuine loving and compassionate intention."

- **Intention Seeds (actions/ habits):** Calendar and call on birthdays, invite friends for coffee, and listen well.

- **Intention Seeds (attitudes):** Be curious and open-hearted in conversation, be present.

- **Stronger body Vision:** "I am growing stronger and healthier day by day."

- **Intention Seeds (actions/ habits):** Take steeper, harder walks, and challenge myself in yoga and gym class.

- **Intention Seeds (attitudes):** Act first, don't wait for motivation, daily gratitude for my incredible body.

I hope these examples show how easy it is to apply the seed-plant-grow approach to any area of your life. You'll notice I've worded the Visions in the present: "I am... I love... Money is..." This is a subtle but important thing to note. It does two things: connects you to your Vision; brings the Vision to the here and now. Wording your Vision as if you are already doing it, being it, living gives your Intention Seeds potency and power.

I love your willingness, sweet bloomer, to Vision your desire in one or more areas of your life and excite yourself with the possibility and potential of Intention Seeds. But, unless we take action, these are just words on a page, or seeds in your pocket. The growth in our LifeGarden happens on the ground, in the everyday steps we take to grow and nurture our desires.

Planting for growth

Once you have clear Intention Seeds, the next step is planting them in action so your dreams and visions start to take root and organically grow.

Practically speaking, taking action might look like:

- Diarising when you'll complete a one-off action or task
- Taking a first step straight away while you have momentum
- Writing out a reminder or mantra for your new attitude shift
- Creating a Cultivate List (that you can use to feed your Daily Planter)
- Making yourself accountable by telling a friend, your partner or a colleague of your intention to take action.

But there's another kind of growth that happens quite organically in the present moment. My experience is that the support from the universe we often speak of is most powerful and clear when *we* are clear about our Intentions.

When I am clear about what it is I am trying to grow when my Intentions are heartfelt and true, magic seems to happen. When I release control of how and when it happens – and exactly what it will look like – life delivers an abundance of opportunities for me to take action in the present moment towards my Intentions.

You might recognise these instances as signs or seedchronicities. Or as a feeling of simply being in flow, in the right place at the right time, when things just seem to come together or finally make sense.

The message I've received most recently from my Goddess in the Garden is that the universe, or life, *loves* when I take action that supports what I need, want and desire. When I first committed to Soul Seed living and began the practice of self-centering regularly, life rewarded me tenfold as if to say, "So glad you're finally listening to your soul's desires… Here, let me help you."

Whatever higher power you resonate with, believe it is here to help you grow yourself and your life. It's both the rain and the sunshine to your LifeGarden. Once you choose to accept that you don't have to *do it all*, that life is helping you cultivate powerful and positive change, you can choose to welcome and embrace this support and guidance.

It's taken me decades of struggle to land here, to realise it's possible to be both the conscious creator of my life and be fully supported by life. It's in my nature, and it's in yours too.

Harvest what grows

Without a doubt, the most richly rewarding part of being a LifeGardener is regularly Harvesting what's growing in yourself and your life as your consciousness and cultivation powers grow.

Harvesting is like having a deeply rich gratitude practice, then taking it wider and deeper into all the areas of your life, all the hidden corners of your LifeGarden. And it's incredibly fun.

Harvesting is a regular reflection practice that allows you to look at everything that has happened within and around you over time. That can be a day, week, month, or even a year.

You can Harvest one specific thing in your life – such as a project you've been working on, a relationship, or an area of your life (a specific garden bed). You can even Harvest *everything* that's happened in your life over time.

Harvesting starts with looking at what's happened, what challenges you've faced and what's grown from your actions, your plantings. But there's a deeper level. Harvesting is about looking at what has grown, changed and blossomed in *you* through these experiences.

What do you now know you don't want to do or be? What do you now know you are capable of? What do you feel drawn to? What do you want more of in your life? What has your Harvest revealed that could enrich your life, your relationships, and your experiences?

Harvesting with your partner, friends or in a group is extremely powerful. When you Harvest with others, you reflect on what you have heard and seen in the other and the power of what each of you Harvest multiplies. As a result, you tend to feel the effects more deeply.

This can be a positive emotional and empowering experience, having someone else, or several others, mirror all that you have overcome, cultivated and become.

I regularly practice Harvesting with two of my closest friends every week, month, and season. We are constantly surprised by the power of reflecting and Harvesting together. Each lesson in self-harvesting is shared and deepened through the sharing.

Harvesting is something I now teach as a fundamental tool in the Ready-Set-Grow programme. I'll talk more about Harvesting later and you can learn more about the RSG programme at the end of the book.

LifeGardening your way

As I mentioned in the introduction, LifeGardening is three things: a philosophy for living, a set of LifeGardening tools, and a process or cycle for cultivating positive and powerful growth and change in yourself and your life.

Just as each new season has its cycles, everything you grow and cultivate will also find its natural rhythm. The art and joy of embracing cultivating your LifeGarden is as much about patience as it is action, as much about planning as it is planting, as much about seeing what's growing now as it is feeling into – in the deepest part of yourself– what you'd truly love to grow next.

In Part seven, I'll bring together all the steps in the LifeGardener Cultivation Cycle. But I want you to remember, more than anything, that there is plenty of room for you to unearth your own unique and powerful way of creating and cultivating your full bloom life.

Even as a seasoned LifeGardener, I am constantly composting, weeding, replanting, creating new garden beds, trying new combinations or co-planting things in my life. The measure of my success is both the joy of the gardening journey – which is deep and rich and never-ending – and witnessing the blossoming of the people and things I feel passionately about as I take responsibility for my personal blooming.

You will find your rhythm, sweet bloomer. You will find your favourite and most natural ways to seed, plant and cultivate. When you do, you'll understand your own blooming was here inside you all along. You've just been waiting for the right conditions. The time is ripe to own your power and cultivate your one deeply rooted, divinely fragrant, full bloom life.

Part Five Harvest

Let's recap what we have grown in Part Five:

- **Seed the change you want to be.** Change – real, full bloom change – only comes from within. Only when we truly envision ourselves living our dreams, and feel ourselves deep within those dreams, can they fully bloom.

- **Compost your past to feed your future.** If we compost the past, rather than let it sit and rot, cause a stench or leave us paralysed with fear, it can enrich the soil of our dreams and desires, remind us of what we do and don't want in our lives and help us grow a better future.

- **Plant Powerful Intention Seeds.** Knowing we can do anything we put our mind and time to, the question becomes, "What do I want to put my heart into?" When we become clear about what's in our heart and what we desire in any area of our life, that Intention becomes nourished with high intensity, love-infused, nutrient-rich superfood.

- **Planting for growth.** Once you have clear Intention Seeds, the next step is planting them in action so your dreams and visions start to take root and organically grow. The universe, is also here to help you grow yourself and your life. It's both the rain and the sunshine to your LifeGarden.

- **Harvest what grows.** Without a doubt, the most richly rewarding part of being a LifeGardener is regularly Harvesting what's growing in yourself and your life as your consciousness and cultivation powers grow.

- **LifeGardening your way** - You will find your rhythm, sweet bloomer. You will find your favourite and most natural ways to seed, plant and cultivate. When you do, you'll understand your own blooming was here inside you all along.

"We delight in the beauty of the butterfly,
but rarely admit the changes
it has gone through
to achieve that beauty."

Maya Angelou

PART SIX

NURTURE

NURTURE

V.

To feed, support and tend to what matters, with love and attention, to enable organic growth and blossoming.

When I first read Scott Pape's *The Barefoot Investor*, I was incredibly inspired by the simplicity of his pathway to freedom and abundance. The seeds of possibility were planted in my heart and mind: financial freedom.

When I shared my relationship seed, plant, grow story in Part five, I lied. My money garden bed was equally overrun with those big, tough weeds of shame, regret and fear.

And, although The Barefoot Investor helped me Vision my future self, my current self needed to start with her feet on the ground, firmly in the soil of her past. I knew the only way to cultivate my financial dreams was to compost my financial past and illuminate the truth about my financial present.

At about the same time I realised I'd never had an intimate relationship, it also dawned on me that I'd never had a healthy and intimate relationship with money. My debts began in my early twenties, I'd never saved for anything in my life, almost claimed bankruptcy twice, been both underpaid and overpaid in my professional life, stolen from supermarket shelves as a teen, and from my parents, pre-teen.

I once opened the door to the local sheriff, who came around to threaten furniture collection in return for unpaid bills. It was my boyfriend's rental, his furniture. Our relationship didn't last long. Not long after, in my thirties, I'd called all my debtors, made agreements, and spent seven years paying off my blacklisted debts.

The seven-year path was long, but with each step, I felt my confidence and self-respect grow. During my single years in my late forties, during my year of self-love and relationship exploration, I also composted my money past. Composting was painful and shameful but incredibly liberating. I knew the only way was down, down, down into the soil of my truth, so I could then grow up towards the sunshine of my future self.

In this part, we'll touch on the importance of cultivating self-trust, especially when you're stuck digging around in the shame of your past and want to start composting that stuff to feed a more positive future. We'll also look at ways to cultivate the three things every woman I know wants more of and needs to flourish: time, energy and support. Finally, I'll share more on the process of visioning and, specifically the LifeGardener Grounded Visioning tool.

With the help of financial feminist and author of *Get Rich, Lucky Bitch,* Denise Duffield Thomas, I dug up my 'money messages', those long-held beliefs around money. If you have never explored the origins of your beliefs around money, do yourself and your kids a favour – it's financial therapy 101.

My whole adult life I had three big dreams when it came to money and making a living:

- Finally, for the first time in my life, weeding out all my debts, planting seeds and watching my savings grow
- Earning a living doing what I love – writing and empowering women
- Buying a beautiful home by the sea.

Why weren't dreams enough? Why hadn't any of this manifested, more than 40 years into my life? I now know there were missing elements that explained why these dreams had never been seeded, let alone grown and bloomed. I want to share these with you because there may be some TruthSeeds inside for you. I call these elements my three money M's.

- 💲 **Message it** – composting my past to uncover the deeply rooted messages that were killing all the nutrients in my soil was non-negotiable. All that grows from negative messages is more weeds. I had to seed brand new money beliefs – Intention Seeds – then actively plant these to see them grow.

- 💲 **Manage it** – managing my money took time each week to step up and face my financial truth, one debt payment at a time. I also used Scott Pape's ridiculously simple (three-bucket) management system to automate the financial flow.

- 💲 **Make it** – most importantly, for the three-bucket system to work, and for the flow of my savings to grow, I needed a regular, reliable income. For more than 12 years, while living in the Blue Mountains and raising my girls, my income had stopped and started, never consistently flowed. At the beginning of 2018, I secured an income that still flows.

It's easy to see how these three elements are interconnected. If I'd worked on my money messaging but not landed a regular steady income flow, I may have felt better about money but not saved a drop. If I'd landed that regular income but not dealt with my money messaging, I would have repeated my past money mistakes, without a doubt.

I hope this is useful for you, sweet bloomer, even if your money garden is nowhere near as weed-infested as mine was. If you do feel just one of these areas resonates with you, then I encourage you to explore it further. I can honestly say adopting the three M's approach to money has allowed me to turn a heavily weed-ridden LifeGarden bed into a full bloom harvest.

In 2018, after securing that regular income, I began chipping away, Barefoot Investor style, at what Scott Pape refers to as 'domino your debts'. I spent that year knocking over $15,000 in personal debts. Guy witnessed that experience and for the first time in my adult life, I was open and honest with my partner about my financial reality and financial dreams.

As the year turned and 2019 dawned, Guy and I began saving together. With all debts behind me for the first time in my life, I turned a financial corner and felt the sunshine of my future warming me with possibility. We created a beautiful Vision together, of buying a house by the ocean at the end of 2021. We calculated two years to grow the big, fat deposit we were keen on.

That year, we had our first ever overseas family holiday – two weeks in New Zealand's South Island – paid upfront. We also paid about $15,000 in unplanned dental and car expenses. Despite the unexpected crises, after saving more than $35,000, we scrambled together a decent deposit to buy our home on the New South Wales south coast in December of 2019, two years earlier than planned.

It was a three-month property settlement, through a season of ravaging bushfires, both at home in the Blue Mountains and by the sea near Cobargo. We watched the fires in the mountains and on the coast with our hearts in our mouths and our car standing ready, evacuation-packed.

On March 18, 2020, we drove the seven hours past blackened forests, signed our papers and put the key in the door of our home for the very first time. I almost collapsed with relief and disbelief. It's hard to describe the feeling in those moments when you're fully conscious of the fact that you are actually living that dream you Visioned.

Composting the past, seeding new Intentions, and growing brand new possibilities with powerful present-moment action... this really was a full bloom Harvest moment.

Nurture self-trust

I may have never cultivated that dream into reality if it wasn't for two vital elements: self-trust and support. Firstly, I needed to trust myself, despite composting a shameful past, to make better choices, take better actions, and grow a healthier garden. I needed to cultivate within myself the belief that now I knew better, I could do better, every single day.

What I came to realise as truth is that deep down underground, the roots of our lives are intertwined and interconnected. It's no coincidence that I began to uncover all the ways I wasn't showing up for intimacy at the same time I was uprooting all the ways I hadn't told myself the truth about money.

If this resonated for you, sweet bloomer, it may be time to trust yourself to look into these truths a little deeper. Trust yourself, trust the process, and trust that when we illuminate our truth, we can liberate ourselves and begin to cultivate a full bloom life.

When I sat in the psychologist's chair and asked, "What do I do next?" she responded with something powerful: "I know you're hesitant about this new relationship, and you feel you can't trust another right now, but you know you have the courage and the wisdom to make better, sometimes harder decisions. You can trust *yourself*."

I want to say the same to you. Trust that you already have all the experience you need, all the wisdom and all the courage to make the decisions you know can replace weeds with flowers. Self-trust is built through tiny, everyday choices and actions. You have a field full of memories from which to Harvest this truth. If there's an area of your life where self-trust is lacking, look out into that field of memories to remind yourself of who you are at your full bloom best.

> **What's in your self-trust field of memories?**
>
> Take a few minutes to think back to the times in your life when you've stepped up and done what you know is right and true. If you were to think of yourself as your own best friend, what are the things you've done for yourself you are most grateful for? Think of the little things and the tough decisions you've made.

Nurture some support

When the time is ripe, when we're fully blooming as women, we come to embrace the truth that all good things are better done together. There is no need for any of us to garden alone, ever. Yet if you're used to playing the victim or martyr (I've played both roles well), it can seem easier to put your head down and just get on with it.

To fully bloom, we all need support along the way. And our blooming is never more beautiful, more appreciated, more precious, than when it is shared with others. Asking for and giving support is what makes us human, lifts us up, fills our hearts and enriches our soil.

I still need to remind myself, three years in, that Guy and I are partners. He'll sometimes say, when I've thanked him for basic help and support, "That's what we do, we're a team." Yet the more I embrace that beautiful truth – I am loved and supported – the richer the experience of it is.

When I was financially down and out, I sought support, guidance, sisterhood, and mentoring. When I needed courage and reflection to step into intimacy, I sought professional help and spent 18 months doing online courses in self-love. When I was woken in the middle of the night in January 2009 by the first of six months of pregnancy panic attacks, I reached out. I spoke to my GP, who referred me to the head psychologist for women at the local public hospital, and I took his advice.

I told everyone in my closest friendship circle and family what I was experiencing, even neighbours, so that if I had an attack and they were around, I knew there was someone who understood. Trying to explain what's going on while you're having a panic attack is almost impossible, especially when you're asked that inevitable question, "What are you panicking about?" There's a chance when they hear the nonspecific answer, 'I'm afraid of everything and anything," they'll freak out too.

As women, we sit at the centre of a circle, surrounded by people who need us, who look to us for energy, love, support, guidance, confidence, courage, wisdom and shelter. Why is it that we give so freely and generously, so naturally, yet we often tend to hesitate at the thought of *receiving* support? Often, we wait until we're desperate, vulnerable and have no choice before we even ask for support.

I'll remind you of what I touched on earlier while discussing self-nourishment, when we seek and obtain what we need to not only survive, but to thrive, we are practising the divine feminine art of receiving.

Way beyond necessity, receiving support has an incredible power to link us together as women so we can rise higher – bloom more fully – than we ever have before. Just days before writing this I watched US Vice President-Elect Kamala Harris stand tall in body and spirit and remind us of this truth.

In one of the most moving speeches in US history, she spoke of standing on the shoulders of the many women who came before her. Then she told the world that in reaching these tremendous history-making heights, she was bringing others with her. In a full-body goosebump moment, she said those unforgettable words: "I may be the first... (and we knew collectively what was coming next)... but I won't be the last."

And she was joyful and elevated, as were her millions of viewers and newly inspired fans around the world. The cameras panned to young girls watching nearby, standing next to their mothers, as she sent them a personal message:

"Because every little girl watching tonight sees that this is a country of possibilities and to the children of our country regardless of your gender, our country has sent you a clear message: dream with ambition, lead with conviction and see yourselves in a way that others may not simply because they've never seen it before."

Kamala was acknowledging the support of those who raised her, who came before her and supported her through their own personal struggle. She chose to pass on the spirit of support through the hearts and minds of those rising around her. What a beautiful moment in time. What a true example of what cultivating support can look like when it comes from the heart with true intention and a divine dose of inspiration.

When it comes to cultivating support for ourselves, our dreams and goals, embracing the attitude of giving and receiving can take our dreams to a whole new level. We'll practice this in Part seven, when we plant our Organic Goals.

But before we move on, let's look at the grass roots level, at what support can look and feel like, because its flowers have many faces:

- **Words of encouragement** – it only takes a few to make a difference. When I was writing this book, just a line or two of encouragement from my mentor, editor or writing friend was all I needed.

- **Asking the right question** – The three most powerful questions I've come across are (in this order): 1. How are you? 2. What do you need? 3. How can I support you in that?

- **Listening space** – we've touched on this already, but I can't say enough about saying nothing. Holding space for someone, with both ears and heart fully open, is a rare and potentially transformative thing. Yet so simple!

- **Prayers and good intentions** – when you can't be in the same space as another, or know they need to walk their own path without your opinion, sending heartfelt prayers and good intentions has a power greater than we may ever rationally understand. Besides, it feels good to do it.

- **Acts of kindness** – any act of kindness, whether from a stranger or not, is a form of support, not just in the physical act itself. Within the act is a reminder that support is not something we need to deserve or earn, but a natural right.

- **Physical support** – helping a struggling mum with eight bags and two kids get into her car, helping a nervous senior cross a busy road, running errands for a tired or unwell friend. Helping lighten the load for another, just for a moment, is a beautiful form of support.

- **Hugs and humour** – at the right time, in the right place, without a doubt hugs and laughs are two of my favourite things. Melting into a hug can transform the sense of urgency and reconnect you to your own sense of okay-ness. And you can't put a price on a good old-fashioned, spontaneous belly laugh.

- **Time support** – millions of volunteers around the world are testament to this truth. But you can also gift time to others by making things easier for them, removing pressure when they're running late, extending a deadline, postponing a coffee or giving them the option to chat on the phone rather than travel to meet.

- **Safety net** – when I told all my neighbours and family about my panic attacks, I felt like I had a huge safety net around me to catch me if I fell. It gave me a sense of security, support and assurance that I have no doubt made a big difference to my ability to cope and sleep at night.

- **Sisterhood and friendship** – It's wonderful to know your friends can be as unique as the support and comfort they provide. Appreciating your friends for exactly who they are and how uniquely they support you is liberating.

- **Professional support** – from accountants to cleaners, to psychologists, to virtual assistants, there is a whole world of support available to help us thrive in our personal and professional lives.

- **Mentoring and guidance** – this book is my fourth attempt in the last 10 years to become a published author. I believe the time was ripe for this one. But I also know it was made possible because of the mentoring I received along the road, and the small circle of women writers who showed up each week in support of themselves and each other. And my biggest fan and greatest support, my partner Guy.

- **Lifelong learning** – education can expand our minds, our resumé and our bank balance. Online learning is peaking, and the variety of content is blossoming. There's never been a greater time to learn anything, anytime. And when we learn together, we all benefit from the strength of our connection and the wisdom of our collective experience.

Nurture your time freedom

You might be wondering why I'd even take the time to talk about cultivating *time freedom*. There are so many myths about the notion of being 'time poor' that can stop us from stepping fully into our power as women. Time spent online, on devices, being 'on' and accessible 24/7 can give the illusion that time in modern western life is one complex web of distraction and fragmentation.

Time poverty is the feeling you get that there is never ever enough time to stop, exhale, down your tools, and go inward. It can cause stress, anxiety, a feeling of lack and a sense of mental and emotional fragmentation.

The reason I'm addressing this here and now with you, dear sweet bloomer, is if you truly want to experience the expansiveness, clarity, and liberation that comes with living your full bloom life, you must begin to shine the light of truth on your own relationship with time. Just like money, if your relationship with time is one of lack and poverty, your life will never feel rich enough, no matter how you're spending your time.

If you're unable to live your life in the present moment, how can you savour the richness of the life you are consciously cultivating? What's the point in being so busy growing and cultivating your life if you have no time to stop and smell the roses?

I've learnt that cultivating time freedom isn't about trying to control, slow or struggle with time. In fact, the key to time freedom can be found deep within our struggles *against* time.

I have a whole book on time freedom bursting to come into bloom, but I wanted to take this book to full flourish and share it with you first. You'll have to wait a little longer for the TimeGardener book.

In the meantime, you can download of copy of the *Power of Presence* eBook series on my website *www.LifeGardener.com.au/free*

It's easy to see how a commitment to cultivating time freedom can help free up your energy. When you begin to embrace the possibility that time is your friend, that other people and life are here to support you, and that you can choose how you react to the time pressures that others hand you, there is immense liberation to be harvested.

Nurture your authentic energy

There is no denying our physical, emotional and mental energy systems are connected. When we're physically unwell, our mood and mental outlook are impacted. When we're feeling joyful and excited, our shoulders lift up and back, and our chest opens. When we're down and depressed, we look downwards, slumping our shoulders, and become slow and heavy in our step.

The beauty of this connection is that if you want to shift or lift your energy, it doesn't matter where you start. You can move the physical body with dance, walking, yoga, qi gong, swimming or any other kind of movement… and eventually the emotional and mental energy systems will follow and be lifted and boosted. You could use your journal to shift your mood, or to talk out your troubles with a friend on a walk, and watch your energy shift and rise as your burden lightens.

This is the beauty of our nature, and of nature itself. It doesn't matter where the shift comes from; as long as the shift brings even a slight change, then energy can flow again. I came to realise a profound truth one day recently while trying to boost my energy following the kidney stone passing: it wasn't so much what I needed to *do* to re-energise… it was figuring out how I could *allow* the energy to flow again.

I needed to get out of my own way, so my energy could resume its natural flow. Yes, I had medical and non-medical assistance. But what my body wanted was to lie flat on my yoga mat, arms skyward in Savasana (surrender) pose and do absolutely nothing, not even plan, several times a day.

I was so interested in energetic healing that I studied some units while at NatureCare College in Sydney in the early 2000s. I trained as a meditation teacher at the time and found there's a never-ending number of ways to shift and work with energy. I have no doubt, sweet bloomer, if you're reading this book, you've probably experienced the benefits of reiki, or massage, or tai chi, or yoga, or other ancient forms of healing.

Whatever your experience of your own mystical and magical energy, you have no doubt lived enough in your wise, energetic body to know when something's just not right, even if you can't put your finger on it.

You know when someone's draining you with their negativity or endless chatter. You know when what someone's saying and what they're thinking are two very different things. You know when it's time for you to leave. You know when you're doing something that every cell in your body doesn't want you to. And you know what feels good in your bones.

Use your wisdom, my sweet and wise friend. Read all the books and take all the courses you want to understand how energy works in the miraculous human body. But most of all, listen to your own body and mind, watch when your energy rises and falls away. This is conscious LifeGardening in energetic action.

Ignoring your body's signs and *soldiering* on is like gardening from a magazine: following feeding and watering instructions and paying no attention to how your plants and flowers are responding. Cultivate a curiosity about your energy, what lifts it, what shifts it, what resonates so beautifully you feel goosebumps in your soul.

Red hot energy

I was once at a Red Hot Chili Peppers concert with my youngest sister. At 16, she was a huge Peppers fan and the tickets scored me sister-of-the-year status! When we arrived at the Sydney Entertainment Centre to crappy seats, the work colleague who had organised the tickets apologised and offered us a spot closer to the action. The upgrade was as close as you could get: the photographer's podium was reserved for media on the front left-hand side of the stage.

As we stood in the pre-concert darkness, the crowd a sweeping hillside of lighters (pre mobile phones), I soaked in the electricity. Kate was almost wetting her pants with excitement. Then she grabbed my arm and pointed down the side of the stage just below us. Anthony, Flea and the other band members were encircled, arms on shoulders, geeing each other up. When they hit the stage, the crowd was unaware, most likely assuming they were yet more roadies moving cords or amplifiers. I gripped Kate's arm with equal force.

Then it happened. The first strum of guitar, the first bright lights. The crowd went wild! I will never forget the electric tsunami that surged from the back row through to the centre of my chest. Wow... I get it now. *This* is why artists perform. This is what feeds all those rock souls and keeps them doing it night after night. Not since seeing Freddie Mercury strut his stuff 10 years earlier had I felt such a powerful surging human force of energy.

Nurture energetic intentions

Back here on earth… in Part two I shared with you my daughter Amy's insights into my need to mind my own business. Following that conversation, I planted myself three powerful Intention Seeds that lifted and shifted my energy:

- **Step back** – take off my superhero cape, stop saving the day for everyone around me (at home and work). The change wasn't instant, but it was nonetheless profound. By pulling back from what wasn't mine to spend energy on, it was like I'd turned my energy from a sprinkler into a beautiful pond. I suddenly had so much more to draw on, and a calmer, deeper sense of my energy and its movements.

- **Step up** – save my energy for the moments when I really need to step up and take action. With my energetic centre now sitting calmly at the heart of my LifeGarden, when I consciously chose to give something my attention and energy, I felt stronger and calmer, able to fully step up.

- **Speak up** – with power and clarity. Saving my energy for what matters also means saving my words and thoughts for what really matters. I found myself speaking less and speaking from a place of authenticity rather than reactivity. Basically, I stopped sticking my nose in other people's business.

Understanding energy and energetic boundaries can save time, energy and LifeGarden growing pains. It can also give those closest to you the opportunity to fully bloom in their own time. When you put time into Harvesting what you know about your energetic self, you begin to experience your full power as the cultivator of your choices and your life. Who you spend time with, what you give energy to, and how you allow yourself to be fully supported; being conscious of what you cultivate for your own growth is essential and empowering.

Part Six Harvest

Let's recap our Nourishing Part Six:

- **The three money M's.** The three actions needed to seed and grow your money dreams - Message it, Manage it, Make it Flow.

- **Cultivating self-trust.** If there's an area of your life where self-trust is lacking, look out into your field of memories to remind yourself of who you are at your full bloom best.

- **Cultivating support.** To fully bloom, we all need support along the way. And no blooming is ever more beautiful, more appreciated or more precious than when shared with others. Asking for and giving support is what makes us human, lifts us up, fills our hearts and enriches our soil.

- **Cultivating time freedom.** When you begin to embrace the possibility that time is your friend, that other people and life are here to support you, that you can choose how you react to the time pressures that others hand you, there is immense liberation to be harvested.

- **Cultivating authentic energy.** Read all the books and take all the courses you want, to understand how energy works in the miraculous human body. But most of all, listen to your own body and mind, watch when your energy rises and falls away. This is conscious LifeGardening in energetic action.

"And the day came when the risk to remain tight in a bud was more painful than the risk it took to bloom."

Anais Nin

PART SEVEN
BLOOM

PART SEVEN

BLOOM

FULL BLOOM LIVING

V.

To live deeply rooted in authenticity,
using daily choices, habits and actions,
to co-cultivate an abundant and meaningful life.

I call this story 'the beautiful rejection', and you'll soon see why.

During the first Covid-19 lockdown in March 2020, when schools began online learning and human movement was limited, we bunkered down in our new home on the New South Wales south coast. Two things soon became clear: firstly, we needed to do some urgent renovation (made obvious when Lily's knee went through the floor while painting a skirting board); secondly, we couldn't afford both our Blue Mountains rental and our new mortgage.

Our original idea was to buy the house and rent it out, but government rumblings of new Covid no-eviction laws were making us nervous. So, we did what all sensible lockdown families did and made a radical decision. Despite having no idea how long homeschooling would last – the government was suggesting six months at that stage – we opted to leave our mountains rental and move ourselves and all our possessions the seven hours from mountains to sea, then see what happened next.

What did happen just as we drove our last load southwards, was a government announcement that senior high schoolers, which included Lily, would be returning to school next Monday, less than a week away. That's when we decided to let Lily get a taste of her lifelong dream of moving out. (I should mention that at the age of three we found her, suitcase packed and one leg out of her bedroom window, heading off to catch the train to visit her friend Bella in Coogee, 90 minutes away).

We landed Lily a fantastic granny flat in the backyard of her best friend's parents. It was the best of both worlds, playing grownups with her bestie, practising cooking and cleaning (sometimes) and getting herself to school, with the security of Hannah's lovely parents nearby. She was to spend six to eight weeks there to give us time to resettle in another Blue Mountains rental.

Three weeks later, just after finishing renovations at the new house on the coast, it was Amy's time to return to school. It was June and paying tenants were now a viable option. We found two beautiful and generous people to move into the upstairs, while keeping the two large downstairs rooms for school holiday weekend visits. It was a perfect scenario.

My original Intention Seed was to give our house, rent-free, to a family impacted by the devastating nearby Cobargo fires. Realistically, we couldn't afford to not receive the rent. As good planting and cultivation would have it, my Intention still sprouted. These tenants had flown in from San Francisco to help rebuild their parents' Cobargo farm, where they'd lost some alpacas, significant numbers of cattle, most of their fencing and their home.

It was an honour to have Matt and Alex move into our house. Even our dog agreed and fell in love with them instantly. With Alex and Matt secured as tenants, Amy and I headed to the Blue Mountains to our first Airbnb. Guy remained on the coast to help our tenants settle in and finalise some renovations.

Over the next six and a half weeks, while Amy attended school in the Blue Mountains, we both hopped between three different Airbnbs while searching for our next rental. I had a clear Vision: *A beautiful Blue Mountains nest for our family to rest and come together for six months before we fly off to our new life on the coast.*

The Airbnb novelty was wearing thin. We applied for six rentals and were painfully rejected every single time. I shared my Vision with my soul sister, Ali, and with Guy, but kept dancing between its divine possibility and the harsh reality. Covid-19 had brought many changes and one of these was that office workers were no longer working in offices. With working and Zooming from home a new reality, the competition for rentals was tough. Not since the late 90s in Glebe, in Sydney's inner west, had I lined up and fought for a rental.

In my sixteen years of living and renting in the Blue Mountains, I had moved four times and always had my pick of the bunch. With each rejection my Vision grew blurry. In my Vision, I'd seen loads of room and light and a beautiful *nest* feel. But growing desperation to reunite the family meant we were applying for tiny, mouldy, miserable places, and still being rejected.

Six weeks in, the clouds parted. Guy posted a desperate plea on Facebook and a friend responded, offering their house for us to rent. When we arrived to look at their place, I had to contain my sheer joy.

It was magnificent, a rambling 100-year-old farmhouse/ashram with a spiral staircase in a crazy tiled floor room, oversized European arched windows, plus a giant ceiling ladder in the rustic kitchen for hanging pots and pans. Rows of citrus and stonefruit, 40 feet of kiwifruit vine, a fire pit, an outdoor eating area and a stone woodfire pizza oven. Chickens to lay us daily eggs, a big, beautiful, friendly dog called Olive, magnolias, wild roses, ancient gum trees and bountiful herbs and greens from the garden.

It gets better. When I first planted the seed with Guy of our Blue Mountains nest, I envisioned it fully furnished. And it was. We had all we needed. Our generous friends were heading off to research their next documentary film and were more than happy for us to use anything we needed.

I'd also committed to myself – planted a big fat Intention Seed – that when we did finally land a rental, I would start writing this book. As I sit and write this part, I'm in one of two cabins on the property made of wrought iron and held up by large trees as pillars. From my writing desk, I look out at a large leaning gum, through a frame of freshly leafed grapevine. To my right, a fruiting fig framed by an oversized window.

It's early November 2020 and in the mornings, I often walk the grounds before writing and savour the beauty of this divine place. I roll citrus flowers and jasmine between my palms to soak in the scent, inspect the fruiting and enjoy all that blooms. I'm bringing pink roses inside daily as a reminder to *soften* and play with the Goddess in the Garden.

This place feels like a dream, and it is. I wanted to share this story with you to demonstrate a divine concept, perhaps the most exquisite part of LifeGardening. When you live your life fully awake, when you plant true Intention Seeds in the rich soil of your dreams and desires, there comes a point when you need to surrender. Because quite often life has a much bigger and better Vision for you.

In this final part I'll bring all we've cultivated together into one beautiful bouquet. We'll harvest all we've learnt about weeding, planting, growing, composting… and plant your first Organic Goals. We'll explore LifeGardening throughout the year, including by the seasons. I'll share with you where you can get your hands on all the LifeGardener tools you need. And we'll finish with a divine dive into this concept of *surrendering*.

But first, back to the beautiful rejection story. In late September we held a sleepover party for Amy's 11th birthday. One of the mothers walked around the estate with me, admiring every little detail but appearing somewhat nervous. She worked in real estate and we were discussing how difficult it had been to find a place. She had shown us one of the six places we were rejected from.

She finally exhaled: "The reason you were rejected is that you had a really bad reference from your last real estate," she said. "Ordinarily I'm not meant to tell you this, but I've just left the industry, so I can."

I nearly fell over. We'd had a heck of a time getting out of our Blue Mountains rental to the coast. Apart from the seven-hour drive, the dishwasher had flooded and damaged the downstairs, as well as the heating duct. Getting out was painful but we'd landed at a good point with the real estate owner, and she'd assured me of a good reference.

When I shared the news with Guy, he was fuming. He started into, "We should call them and…" and I turned to him.

"Honey, look where we are. Who cares why or how it happened? If it hadn't taken six weeks of looking and losing out, we may not have landed right here. What a beautiful rejection!"

Cultivate your power

Being a LifeGardener gives you the freedom and ability to:

- Compost your past to feed your future
- Weed out what's not working in your life
- Plant powerful Intention Seeds with new actions, habits, beliefs and attitudes
- Self-nourish so you can move beyond surviving to thriving
- Grow your dreams and desires from the fertile soil that feeds your soul

What I want to invite you to explore now is what a full bloom life looks and feels like for you. My hope is that these thoughts and feelings have already begun blossoming within your heart, body and mind.

My heartfelt wish is that this book, its philosophy and tools, help you to see, feel and embrace the divine beauty of your unique self, and feel the blooming potential of self-liberation and full feminine power.

My Soulful Intention, each time I write to you, or connect with you online or in life, is to meet you in the heart space, leave my ego at the door (as much as is humanly possible), and reflect like a mirror of truth your divine essence back to you.

The mantra below has followed me all my conscious life, for at least the last 30 years. I have felt its power several times along my life journey.

The freedom to be, the wisdom to see, all that you are and can be.

I believe it was created by my soul for me, and for the 'soul work' I am meant to do in the world. I'm sharing it with you now, from my heart and soul to yours.

PART SEVEN: BLOOM

◆

Want to explore your full bloom life?

Grab your journal and pen for a moment and explore your full bloom life. Use the prompts below if they help bud fresh ideas:

- What makes up the rich soil of your deepest dreams and desires?
- Where is your sunshine?
- Where is your Goddess in the Garden right now and what does she crave more than anything?
- If you could start with any part of your life – any garden bed – which one would you weed and replant first?
- If you could plant three magic Intention Seeds right now, that were guaranteed to grow, what would they be?
- What would your full bloom LifeGarden look like?
- How do you feel when you see and imagine yourself in the middle of that garden, tasting the sweet nectar and harvesting the fruits of everything you have done, learnt and become?

I believe all you see and feel is possible, plant-able. I believe the more we feed our dreams and desires, the clearer and more beautiful our LifeGarden path becomes. I believe questions are even more important than answers.

I believe in the power of exploration and cultivation, of presence and potential. When we come to understand that we can seed, plant and grow our life into full authentic bloom, we have no other work to do than be our most authentic blooming self.

Plant organic goals

When we set ourselves New Year's resolutions or goals, and they don't manifest, the results can be disappointing or even devastating. It's easy to feel like a failure for not having the discipline to see things through, to keep our promises to ourselves.

But life isn't linear, and we change and grow all the time, so why shouldn't our goals? And when we create our goals only with our mind, not our heart, then our heart isn't in it.

So, what's the difference in planting organic goals using the LifeGardener approach? Basically, the process is much richer, more meaningful and super powerful. Organic (LifeGardener) goals:

- Grow and change with you
- Are planted in the fertile soil of your heart and soul's desire
- Are grounded in your current reality

I'll walk you through the basic steps here to give you a clearer understanding. These steps give you a basic look at the much deeper process I've created as part of the **Ready-Set-Grow** Programme (more on this later).

> *Step 1* – **Create your garden beds**
> Your garden beds are where you want to focus your attention and consciously grow your goals for the future. These could be things like money and wealth, career or business, friendships, learning and education, passion projects, hobbies or interests, travel and adventure, family and friends.

Step 2 – **Ground yourself in truth**
There is no point in setting goals on the horizon of your life if your feet aren't firmly grounded in the soil of your own reality. This could be as simple as asking yourself some Blooming Questions like, "How am I travelling in this area of my life? How do I feel about this area of my life?"

Step 3 – **Find the words**
Write down, for each of your garden beds, what changes you want to make, and what you want to experience in these areas. This is only a draft of your goal wording. You could even just do dot points or thought bubbles if you wish.

Step 4 – **Create a Vision**
For each of your garden beds, take some time to get quiet, close your eyes and imagine yourself living that goal. See yourself in it, bringing it to life. Stay with this until you can feel the experience in your body. When you open your eyes, write down what you saw and felt. The visioning often brings a rewrite of your goal, sometimes a completely fresh one.

Step 5 – **Write your Intention Seeds**
While your goal and Vision are fresh, write down anything you intend to do to make that goal a reality. This can include actions, new habits, or a new attitude or approach. Keep writing until you feel done.

Step 6 – **Plant in action**
Take a look at your Intention Seeds and choose one or two things you could take action on now, to plant the seeds of your goal and let them take root.

Step 7 – **Diarise what's next**
Take a look at your Intention Seeds. Is there anything more likely to grow if you schedule it on a future date or as a regular action? Plant it now.

In my previous life, I'd set goals that just wouldn't grow, either because my heart wasn't in it, I gave up, or it felt like way too much work – like pushing against the odds. In these past few years, the goals I've planted at the beginning of the year (usually late January), have ripened in their own perfect time and perfect way.

What's interesting is that I rarely look at them throughout the year while I'm harvesting, planting, growing and intention seeding. Yet, when I do occasionally glance back at them, I realise they are manifesting within my life. Sometimes one or two may have fallen away, because I outgrew them. In most cases, I have grown something even richer.

When I teach people how to Vision powerfully, and they experience how it feels in their body and heart to live their future now, the result is both powerful and magical.

Remember, as beautiful as your Vision may be, life often has a bigger, more beautiful, more bountiful one in store for you, just waiting to bloom if you're willing to surrender control.

So, once your goals are created, there's an element of releasing to nature the timing and ripening of your dreams, goals and desires. Remember, life and the universe are the sunshine and the rain.

There are many reasons organic LifeGardener goals tend to manifest. What's of most interest to me in this process – apart from the sunshine and the rain – is that, although life and circumstance change constantly, what matters most rarely does. That's reflected in the authentic way organic goals are created, from the soil of your heart and soul's longing and with feet firmly grounded in your reality.

The other thing that has brought great power to my yearly organic goal planting process these past two years is the Harvesting that comes before it.

Harvesting the year that was

The first time I did this I was completely blown away. It was the end of 2019, and I had no idea where to start, or whether I would remember everything that happened that year. But I did. I began slowly.

I wrote the areas of my life on LifeGardener inspired flower drawings, (this LG dream has been a long time coming): love and relationships, wealth and value, knowledge and wisdom, health and happiness, fun, joy and adventure.

Once I began the process flowed. I asked myself questions like:

- What happened in 2019?
- What grew from my experiences?
- What did I learn about myself?
- What do I now know I desire more than anything?
- What do I need to feel balanced and nurtured?
- What is blossoming within me?
- What can I do to support myself better in 2020?

And these were all valuable questions and explorations. As we all know, 2020 was a huge year. As the calendar flipped, the bushfires raged in the Blue Mountains where we were renting and on the south coast where we had just bought. Covid-19, known only as Coronavirus at that stage, was a distant and remote disease confined to China and the small corners of the nightly news.

Guy and I were freshly engaged, and I sat at my first-ever climate change protest in the busy streets of Sydney with thousands of other normal everyday activists blocking traffic and angering disrupted motorists. Greta Thunberg was rising to great heights, despite attempts to pull her down.

Life was hot and intense, and we had no idea what was ahead of us.

Now and then, I ask Lily or Guy to Harvest with me all that happened in that two years. We always ended up in awe and often fits of laughter at the almost absurd experience that has been life since the end of 2019.

But the richness that comes from Harvesting goes way beyond what's happened. To me the *what's happened* is a long, broad look at the events of the past. When you drop deeper and go vertical, that's when the layers of life get richer. The richness of our experiences comes not just from what we've faced but how we've responded, what we've learnt, what's grown in us.

Harvesting helps you make sense of events, gain perspective, and spend some time *in the sunshine,* feeling into all that you are and have become along the way. And when you share your Harvest, the celebration or recognition you feel deepens from the shared experience.

The other thing that happens at the end of your yearly Harvest is that you fully arrive in your present-day reality, because you have fully received the lessons and experiences of your past in every cell of your being.

You can see why experiencing an annual Harvest can add great power to the process of planting organic goals. When you Harvest first, you really are starting from a place of deep, authentic truth.

Just as a gardener harvests what's growing and considers what to plant and prune with the turning of each season, so it is for the LifeGardener. A gardener observes and learns from what the garden has to teach them. The LifeGardener observes and learns what this season of their life has brought, and consciously chooses what to plant for the season to come.

The two annual Harvests I have so far experienced – at the end of 2020 and 2021 – have been richly rewarding. Despite the extreme challenges these two years brought, in fact, because of them, I had so many significant events to reflect upon. There was an abundance of opportunities for growth, so many things that I faced and grew from, and so many things and people to be grateful for in my life.

The most powerful insights with both these annual Harvests came with the realisation I had consciously cultivated my life in a garden of unknowns. I had taken small steps and made big choices at a time when it was easy and understandable to fall into fear, paralysis and inaction. I know how transformative this has been for me – and for those in my closest circle – and now I want you to feel the power of your own personal transformation too.

The LifeGardener Cultivation Cycle

Throughout this book, I've shared with you the LifeGardener tools and ways to use them. We've looked at setting intention seeds, weeding what's not working, composting your past to feed your future, planting your seeds in action, visioning and harvesting.

In the **Ready-Set-Grow** Programme, I dig into how to deepen these practices and connect them through the LifeGardener Cycle. Every

LifeGardener tool has a power of its own. The Cultivation Cycle allows you to bring a rhythm to the process and make the most of each of these tools.

It will be clear to you now, how each of these tools in the cycle feeds into the next.

- Harvesting what's grown helps 'shake the seeds' for what's next.
- Visioning brings power to your Intention Seeds because you've seen and felt deeply into your desires.
- When you plant your actions, they're more likely to take root because you're planting the intention seeds which came from your seen and felt vision, which came from the harvest.

When it comes to helping your garden grow, you're aware that true organic growth is powered equally by what you do – how you tend your garden through observation and action – and the degree to which you allow life and the universe to provide support (rain and sunshine).

LifeGardening by the seasons

While living in the Blue Mountains, when autumn came around, I always felt a natural desire to let go of the things I felt weren't serving me in my life. It was a metaphorical connection to the changing colours and falling leaves that surrounded me.

When the days grew shorter in winter, I felt a natural desire to do less, to expect less from myself in my workday and to feed and nourish my body and mind with hearty foods, early nights and fireside conversations.

When you live in a place with distinct seasons, the environmental changes bring a change in mood, energy and desire. For those already seeing the merging of the seasons with climate change, or those living in more temperate or unique climates, these changes aren't as distinct.

Whatever your seasonal experience, there's a lot to be gained from setting powerful Intention Seeds with each season or cycle, then Harvesting what grows and shows and resetting Intentions for the season that follows. It gives a sense of rhythm and allows for consciousness and adjustment. It gives us a chance to check in with our organic goals, see how they're growing, what needs more, or less, feeding and watering.

I love the notion that much of the time, things will grow and bloom simply because we give them the right amount of attention when it is needed. We don't have to constantly watch flowers for them to bloom. Likewise in our own lives, once we've planted Intention Seeds and they've taken root, we don't need to supervise them for them to grow.

In fact, there's nothing more beautiful than being surprised when you look at a garden bed within your LifeGarden and see something beautiful has emerged. What makes seasonal Harvesting so powerful is its authenticity. You're creating Intentions just before a season starts, based on what's growing in you and around you at that time.

Sharing your intentions and harvest

Seeding, planting and growing your full bloom life is so much more powerful when you share the experience. The power in the process seems to be multiplied when you share your Intentions, speak them out loud, and then reflect on each other's Harvest. As I mentioned earlier, when you share your Harvest, it's made more bountiful and beautiful.

I continue to share the Intention Seed setting and Harvesting process with a growing circle of women. I decided as this circle expanded, I wanted to open the door for many other women to experience this powerful process, to set Intention Seeds and to Harvest each month and season together, so we can reap the Harvest collectively!

There's more information about the **Full Bloom Cultivation Circle** – for graduates of the **Ready-Set-Grow Programme** – on my website. I'll share more about this at the end of the book.

Shining the light – Goddess in the Garden

In Part four I introduced you to the Goddess in the Garden, the softest, wisest part of the self. In essence, she is the doorway to presence through your senses, the key to spending more of your life as a human *being*, not just a human doing.

More importantly, she has shown herself to me as the essence of joy, the abundance of deeply rich living. She Visions, she guides, she intuits.

I want to help you explore, embrace and embody her power within you. What's come to light in me is that she requires her own separate book: *The Goddess and The Gardener*. The writing has begun, and I look forward to sharing her with you when she is ripe for the picking.

Your Goddess Gardener self will be the one who shows you all the ways your life is coming into full bloom. Only through her can you savour the sweet surrender of all that's growing and showing within and around you. She is the one who celebrates your Harvest with you and bursts your heart open with gratitude and tears in those divine moments when you realise your power, and when you recognise the beauty of all that you are and all you create and cultivate.

Now that I know you understand *her* essence and power, I want to share with you the three ways my Goddess in the Garden has shone the light on my LifeGarden. My hope and Intention is that these Illuminate some truth for you, provide a sense of clarity and liberation, and help you cultivate your own full bloom life.

ONE
Lighting the path

We began this book from a point of truth. That when we shine the light of truth on what's happening both inside and around us, we Illuminate our authentic truth. Self-truth is always the starting point.

It's true also that this illumination helps guide us on our path ahead. When we LifeGarden, we stay conscious and fully awake to where we've been, where we're going and what's feeding that desire. Truth and authenticity are the guiding lights for each natural next step we take. And only when we are fully present and listening to our softest self – our Goddess in the Garden – can we be led by light.

Even when the future is unknown – and it always is, not just during these Covid-19 years – when you're fully conscious, it's enough to see the natural next step is right in front of you. You can trust that just by taking that next step, and only when you take it, the next one will appear.

TWO
Living in light

I set an intention when writing this book, that I would write *in light*. What that meant for me was I would show up at the keyboard with absolute presence, focus, and devotion to you, sweet bloomer. I would do all I could to get out of my way, to leave the ego at the door and write from the heart. I created a ritual of lighting a candle each time I wrote. As the book grew and my Goddess in the Garden did more of the writing, I began to walk through parts of the physical garden before I sat to write.

I share this with you because I believe we can set a similar intention in any area of our lives. Living in light is living in love, where our Goddess lives all the time. Living in light is a simple choice we can make at any given moment. When I found it hard to put this into practice in certain areas of my life because I wasn't feeling the love, I'd ask myself, "What would love do now? Where in your life can you live with more light?"

THREE
Living with lightness

Finally and most beautifully, my Goddess in the Garden has shown me it's possible to live this very busy, very full, very serious life differently... with lightness. It's a terrific reminder for the control-freak Virgo part of myself who sometimes needs a gentle nudge, or a frank life lesson from her daughter, to step back, take a breath and respect my energetic boundaries.

As recently as September 2021, it was my Goddess in the Garden who guided me to self-centre and to live more authentically from my SoulSeeds, to prioritise what my soul desired most of all. It was her lightness that reminded me that Grace and Ease are my path to peace.

PART SEVEN: BLOOM

Your LifeGardener path

It's easy to find yourself deeply inspired or energised by a book and – like a good holiday – to forget all about it when it ends. It's true, LifeGardening is a philosophy, a shift in consciousness, and a set of tools to help you cultivate a richer, deeper, more meaningful life rooted in authentic truth. I hope you don't just put this book back on the shelf and walk away from its invitation.

There are two garden paths you can choose from here, my sweet bloomer. Which one are you drawn to walk down?

PATH 1

I want to THINK like a LifeGardener

- I know my past can be composted to feed my future
- I know I can weed out what's not working in my life
- I know I can plant new ideas and beliefs – Intention Seeds
- I know I need to self-nourish for my life to flourish
- I know when I'm clear about what really matters to me – my dreams and desires – I can grow my LifeGarden from this rich soil.

PATH 2

I'm ready to BE a LifeGardener

- ꧁ Step into my power as a conscious cultivator of my life
- ꧁ Seed and plant powerful Intention Seeds in the soil of my soul's desires
- ꧁ Self-nourish to flourish by feeding my needs and wants so I can truly thrive
- ꧁ Consciously compost my past to feed my future
- ꧁ Set Intentions each season and Harvest when the time is ripe
- ꧁ Embrace my Goddess in the Garden and follow her light and wisdom
- ꧁ Love LifeGardening and savour the sweet nectar and bounty it brings.

If you're thinking like a LifeGardener already, that's wonderful! If you're feeling drawn to the path of *living* as a LifeGardener, that's blooming beautiful!!

Whichever garden path you choose, the benefits are bountiful. Imagine what we can create within our sisterhood, our family, our workplace, our neighbourhood, our world when we truly step into a new, abundant approach to living.

My dream is that this book brings a flourishing of possibility, that we realise as women in our full bloom power that positive change is not only possible, but inevitable, when it's grounded in the soil of collective soulful desire. When enough of us desire heartfelt change, and we're living proof it is possible, only great things can grow.

I trust we can live deeply rooted in what matters and be fed and led by light along our path. Let's practice this within ourselves, and within our LifeGardener community, then spread the Seeds of possibility we have grown from our collective Harvest.

Come LifeGarden with me…

CONCLUSION

Final flourish – blooming magical journey!

As I reflect on everything we've covered, a divine realisation has blossomed. This book has been seeded, planted and grown LifeGardener style. I want to share its simple blooming story with you to demonstrate the power of choosing the path of least resistance (control) to cultivate what you most desire.

See, I've long dreamt of writing many books. I've started a few. But only this one has grown to full bloom harvest (so far, sweet bloomer). So, what did I do differently to make this dream a reality? I was no less busy than with previous attempts.

There were no less physical or emotional obstacles. In the six weeks I wrote it I passed a kidney stone, took two 'weak weeks' to recover, wept as my daughter moved out, sliced my number two right toe, juggled my full-on fulltime job and got on with the everydayness of life.

I want to harvest the lessons – for myself and you – and revisit the LifeGardener steps I took and choices I made, that made this book bloom:

- **Start with a simple, clear Intention** – when the idea of the book was Seeded, I committed to planting it, by sitting and writing as soon as we found our mountain nest for my family to settle into.

- **Create a beautiful Vision** – in the weeks before I began writing, I started to visualise typing the final words (as I am now), holding my first printed copy and joyfully sharing it with women around the world.

- **Grow in fertile soil** – I put my heart and soul into this book because it grew from the soil of my deepest dreams and desires, to be a published author, to connect with women around the world and to start a conversation that could change the way we view it and live in it.

- **Plant in action** – most importantly, I showed up, did the work, and took the action. And my actions were powered by my desires, my dreams, and my Vision.

- **Cultivate support** – the biggest difference between this one and my previous book attempts is that I cultivated an abundance of support. I shared my book dream with Guy and my girls, so they supported my writing time 100%. I had accountability, professional support and a cheer squad in my writing mentor, six other women writing in tandem over six weeks and a very generous and supportive editor. I deliberately kept my support circle small, keeping the book a secret, so I didn't open myself up to criticism and spend more time answering questions than writing.

- **Plant a new habit with a ritual** – I was so excited when I realised, just after moving to our mountain nest, I could retreat to the wrought iron cabin to write. In the hundred or so steps from the house to the cabin, I dropped into my writing zone, lit my candle and committed to the keyboard, free of internet disruptions.

- **Invite the Goddess in the Garden** – I realised as I wrote that my Goddess had a huge role to play in awakening my sensual self in the (real) garden at the mountain nest and finding the voice of my heart, not just my head.

- **Harvest what's grown** – During each of the six weeks of writing, I had to submit a section for feedback and editing. This made Harvesting what was growing a regular and powerful experience. I also harvested with Guy, Ali and my mentor Emma when I felt truly inspired along the journey.

- **Compost the past** – as I wrote, all the doubt demons came out to play, telling me I was wasting my time, there's a reason why I've never come this far before. Understandably, my money and relationship past also reappeared, and I composted the lot as I wrote, some of which I shared with you.

- **Self-Nourish to Flourish** – I have a history of workaholism and like most women, I can push myself hard when I have a deadline. This time I knew if I was going to walk the talk, I'd have to stay soft. I allowed myself to be pulled and inspired, not pushed and driven. This meant looking after myself well, doing all I could to move from survive to thrive. And today, as I step over the finish line of my first draft, I'm dancing, not falling. Even I'm surprised and delighted by that!

You were my Intention

This whole blooming magical journey was made possible because of you. You were my guiding light, my morning sun. I didn't just write this book for you, I wrote it with you right next to me, across the table… sometimes with a cup of tea, sometimes a glass of wine.

I want to thank you for being here in spirit before you even knew this book existed. This is the magic and beauty of cultivation, of LifeGardening. We are creators, birthers, manifestors, gardeners, cultivators. And our power to cultivate flourishes when we hold ourselves and each other in our heart.

Covid-19 taught us we don't need to be at the table to connect with each other. Writing this book has shown me the power of connecting in spirit, although I dream of meeting you soon, face to face and heart to heart. As I write, a beautiful Vision is growing in my mind. Here's what I see:

A garden with a large rustic table, a generous bounty of fresh food, water bowls and floating flowers, women chatting and laughing, sharing stories, some seated at the table, others on cushioned carpets around the luscious garden. It's a gathering of women who have chosen to come together in celebration of all they have created and will create, some alone, some together.

They have fully stepped into their power to seed, plant and grow their own lives. Now they're ready for more. We're here to seed even bigger changes in the world…

I know this Vision is mine for now. But I wanted to share it with you now, organically, in the moment. Receiving a Vision is a beautiful thing. Sharing a Vision can allow it to grow even richer, and more beautiful. I have no doubt my Goddess in the Garden gifted me that Vision.

For now, sweet bloomer, the time feels ripe to say goodbye. May the soil of your soul be deep and rich, your Intentions be seeded, your full bloom Harvest be bountiful, and your Goddess in the Garden be wild and free.

THE END

EPILOGUE

On June 1, 2021, I almost died. I climbed a cliff edge I shouldn't have and found myself halfway up, perched on a crumbling ledge with Guy on the rocks below, fretting. For the longest few minutes of my life, I held on, not knowing how to go up or down without falling to the jagged rocks below.

It's the first time in my life I've felt there was no way out; I was about to fall to my death. I recall moments of beauty within the fear. I looked across the shimmering ocean to Mt Gulaga in the distance, then spotted a dolphin close to shore and an eagle up high. Then I flashed to my girls, my family and Guy below.

I wasn't choosing to die. I wanted to stay. I didn't know how to save myself.

Then it happened. Guy pushed himself up from the rocks below, high enough to give my right foot a strong push, before sliding back down. The push was the momentum I needed. I knew this was it – my chance to live.

I scrambled high enough to grab the grass roots at the top of the cliff, then dragged myself up to safety. I lay on the grass staring at the sky, unable to stand let alone look over the cliff edge.

In the weeks that followed, Guy and I had to come to terms with what happened. I ended up calling it my Eagle moment; my fall or fly moment. In an effort to derive meaning and significance, I vowed to myself I'd spend more time with people I love and doing the things most meaningful to me.

Almost nine months later, in a phone conversation with two friends, I was asked how my LifeGardener book and business were coming along. I started complaining about all the things that were getting in the way and delaying my business and my dreams from fully blooming.

I complained about my full-time job – the job I'd been talking about resigning from for the last nine months so I could step into self-employment and enjoy autonomy and freedom. When one of my friends asked when I was resigning, I told them June 1, 2022 – three months away – felt like perfect timing; a full circle Eagle moment.

Then my friends did something not all friends can do; they called me out. They held a mirror up to me and my false struggles, my weak excuses for not acting now. Why wait? What's the delay? You've been saying you're ready for so long.

It was hard to hear, and even harder to feel. Was I really delaying my own blooming? Was I letting false struggles and small fears keep my life small, my LifeGarden from blossoming? Isn't this what I'm wanting to teach others?

In the days that followed the truth of their words permeated all corners of my LifeGarden. I realised life had been calling me to step up in my parenting, my relationships, my health, my job, and my business.

The false struggles were like deeply rooted weeds that I'd planted in my own garden, then whinged and complained they were just too difficult to move. But I started weeding, calling myself out, and taking the actions – both big and small – to bring more abundance and beauty to my relationships and into my life.

As a LifeGardener, I've created clear and powerful Visions for my full bloom life and business. I was doing the work and taking the steps to bring those Visions to life. I was growing my full bloom reality. What I forgot to do was keep an eye on the weeds of fear – the false struggles – that were holding me back. It took a mirror from my friends to shatter the illusions and break free.

Just two weeks after the phone call I resigned. That same morning, I found this on social media:

"I have come to accept the feeling of not knowing where I am going.

And I have trained myself to love it.

Because it is only when we are suspended in mid-air with no landing in sight, that we force our wings to unravel and alas begin our flight.

And as we fly, we still may not know where we are going.

But the miracle is in the unfolding of the wings.

You may not know where you're going, but you know that so long as you spread your wings, the winds will carry you."

C. Joybell C.

You don't need an Eagle moment to help you rise above your limitations. But sometimes a higher perspective can help you see what's growing in your LifeGarden. If you find a load of weeds, know that you have the strength to rip out the weeds and find the flowers beneath. As your garden comes into full bloom, so will you!

About the Author

Lyndal Edwards is a Life Enrichment teacher and author living on the far south coast of New South Wales, Australia. Lyndal is the founder of the **Ready-Set-Grow Life Enrichment Program,** where she teaches women the tools for cultivating positive and powerful change in themselves, their life, and the world.

She is also the cultivator of the **Full Bloom Cultivation Circle,** which brings women together to seed their intentions and share what they are harvesting, in line with the moon cycles and the turning of the seasons.

Lyndal is devoted to helping women ignite their passion for life, by seeing life as a garden that can be cultivated and enriched. Lyndal seeded the LifeGardener metaphor in late 2019 and began using its tools in early 2020, as Covid-19 brought chaos and confusion. When it felt like the world was tilting on its axis, Lyndal began 'planting' the natural next steps for herself and her family.

What grew was a powerful way to not only cope with the unknowns of the pandemic, but to live from a point of cultivation rather than control.

She's a trained meditation facilitator and uses meditation and grounding practices in much of her live and online work. She writes passionately on several subjects, including self-liberation, feminine productivity, authentic living, the power of presence, cultivating change and life enrichment.

She is influenced and inspired by the work of Glennon Doyle, Sara Wilson, Brene Brown, Deepak Chopra, Eckhart Tolle, Gabrielle Bernstein, Elizabeth Gilbert and Maya Angelou, among others.

Acknowledgements

Guy Fordy, for his humour and love

Amy Reynolds, for her creativity and wisdom

Lily Reynolds, for her strength and courage

Marsha Edwards, for her humour and willingness

Rowena Edwards, for her insights and devotion

Alison Nancye, for her inspiration and honesty

Miriam Joy-Jones, for her authenticity and joy

Emma Franklin-Belle, for her Manuscript Mastery

Maria Chavez, for her energy and design devotion

Amanda McPaul, for her sunshine and cover art

Tia Fereti, for her luscious illustrations

Michael Joy and Mieke Clare, for the divine writing studio

Miss Payne, my year 3 teacher, for her encouragement

My sisters, for their sisterhood

My dog Finn, for his company and loyalty

Connect with the author

- 🌐 LifeGardener.com.au
- ✉ info@lifegardener.com.au
- 📷 lifegardener_with_lyndal/
- f facebook.com/LifeGardener.with.Lyndal
- ▶ tinyurl.com/33xt7kta

Download your FREE Book Bonuses

Your 'Daily Planter' - Video + PDF
Try the Organic + Abundant LG Daily to-do list!

Divine Summer Goddess Meditation – Mp3
Shift from Doing to Being!

Power of Presence eBook

Deepen Your Relationships

Invite More Joy & Peace

Improve Your Energy

Find them all at
www.lifegardener.com.au/free

Want To Explore The Lifegardener Path?

Find out more about the:
Ready-Set-Grow Life Enrichment Program
&
Full Bloom Cultivation Circle

www.lifegardener.com.au

Ready-Set-Grow Life
Enrichment Program

Learn and practice being a LifeGardener

༄

Seed plant and grow your full bloom life

LIFE ENRICHMENT AUTHOR & TEACHER-LYNDAL EDWARDS

www.ingramcontent.com/pod-product-compliance
Lightning Source LLC
Chambersburg PA
CBHW010706020526
44107CB00082B/2693